THIRD UNIT
SHOP
STORAGE

PLAYROOM

BATH

SECOND UNIT

BEDROOM

CARPORT
FINISH GRAVEL AT ELEV. 98'-0"

FACIA LINE

DRAWING LINE

HOSE BIBB

PERFORATED BOARD
SEE DETAIL
(SHEET 6).

R NOTE: ALL INTERIOR DOORS TO BE CONSTRUCTED
OF VERTICAL BOARDS SAME AS, AND FLUSH WITH,
INTERIOR WOOD PARTITIONS.
SIZES AS NOTED.

COATS

6'-6"

6'-2" SOFFIT

HOSE BIBB

PERFORATED
BOARDS
(SEE DETAIL)

⊕ LIGHT OUTLET ON CEILING OR

⊠ OUTSIDE PHONE

⊡ DOOR BELL BUTTON. ED

■ NOTE LETTER BY SWITCH RE
LETTER BY LIGHT OUTL

CONCRETE

■ CONTRACTOR SHALL PROVIDE A
PLETE ALL PARTS OF THE BU
NECESSARY FOR THE PROPER
ALL SLABS, FOOTINGS, FOUND V

■ PROVIDE ALL REINFORCEMENT
AND SET AND FIT IN PLACE. P
ETC. FORM AND CONSTRUCT ALL
BRING ABOUT THE PROPER C

■ SET IN CORRECT PLACES ALL
CHORS, ETC. NEEDED TO SECUR

■ ALL CONCRETE FOR FLOORS
PART PORTLAND CEMENT TO
AND ONE-HALF PARTS HARD, WAS
SO FOR STEPS. CONCRETE FOR
ONE PART CEMENT, THREE PAR
GRAVEL. CONCRETE FLOORS, UN
FORCED WITH ONE LAYER OF 6
SHALL BE INTEGRALLY FINISH
SURFACE AND MARKED ¾" DEEP
SHOWN ON DRAWINGS. ALL CON
GRALLY COLORED WITH APPRO
SIMILAR TO RED COLORUNDUM
N.Y.

■ CONCRETE CONTRACTOR SHALL
TECTION OF HIS WORK, AND SH
CLEAN AND FREE FROM STAINS
OF THE FINAL COMPLETION OF T

■ CONCRETE CONTRACTOR SHALL
BARS AND MESH AS SHOWN IN A
UM GRADE (DEFORMED) STEEL R

MASONRY

■ PROVIDE ALL LABOR AND MATER
DICATED AS MASONRY INCLUDIN
HEARTHS, STONE FLOORS, COPING
ANGLES, ANCHORS, CLAMPS, ETC,
AND ALSO INCLUDING ALL SCAFF
CONSTRUCTION OF STONE WORK.

■ ALL MASONRY WALLS, STEPS, ETC,
BRACED TIGHT WOODEN FORMS
WALL FACES PREVIOUS TO FILLIN
ALL CONCRETE SHALL BE MIXED
PORTLAND CEMENT TO THREE PA
ED GRAVEL OR HARD CRUSHED
LY VIBRATED AND TAMPED, SO AS
OF VOIDS AND HOLES, ETC.

■ CONTRACTOR SHALL PROVIDE AN
RY WALLS, PARAPETS, CHIMNEYS, M
ED TO THE CONTRARY. REINFORCI
CALLY AND HORIZONTALLY IN TW
2½" CLEAR OF WALL FACES. ANC
LAYER OF REINFORCING. ANCHOR
TENDING OVER ½" Ø EACH SIDE

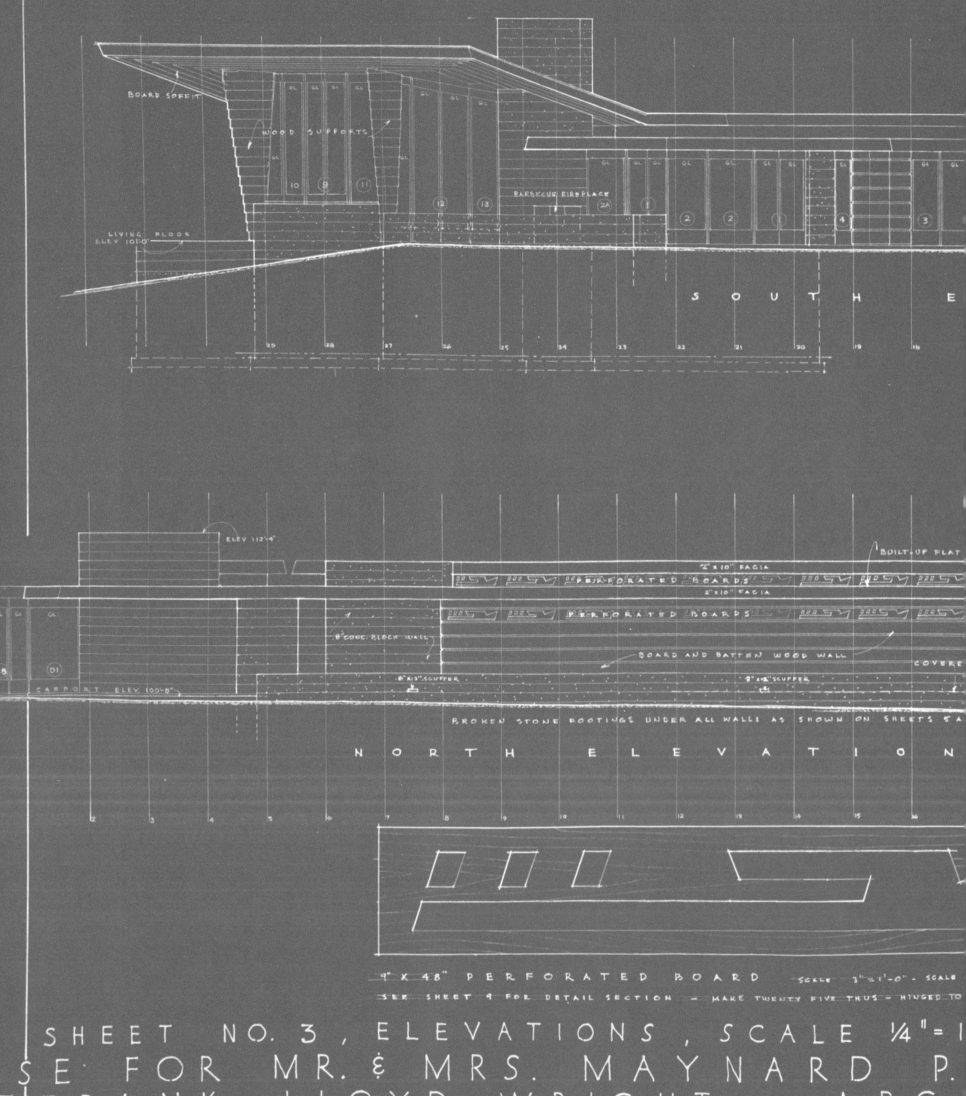

BOARD SOFFIT

WOOD SUPPORTS

GL GL GL

10 9 11

GL

12 13

BARBECUE FIREPLACE

2A 1

GL GL GL GL GL GL GL GL GL

2 2 1 4 3

LIVING FLOOR
ELEV 101'-0"

S O U T H   E

29   28   27   26   25   24   23   22   21   20   19   18

ELEV 112'-4"

BUILT-UP FLAT

2" x 10" FACIA

PERFORATED BOARDS

2" x 10" FACIA

PERFORATED BOARDS

8" CONC. BLOCK WALL

BOARD AND BATTEN WOOD WALL

COVERE

GL

D1

8"x12" SCUPPER

8"x12" SCUPPER

CARPORT ELEV. 100'-8"

BROKEN STONE FOOTINGS UNDER ALL WALLS AS SHOWN ON SHEETS 5A

N O R T H   E L E V A T I O N

2   3   4   5   6   7   8   9   10   11   12   13   14   15   16

9" X 48" PERFORATED BOARD   SCALE 3"=1'-0" · SCALE

SEE SHEET 9 FOR DETAIL SECTION · MAKE TWENTY FIVE THUS · HINGED TO

S H E E T   N O. 3 ,   E L E V A T I O N S ,   S C A L E   ¼" = 1

S E   F O R   M R. & M R S.   M A Y N A R D   P

F R A N K   L L O Y D   W R I G H T ,   A R C

FRANK LLOYD WRIGHT
on the West Coast

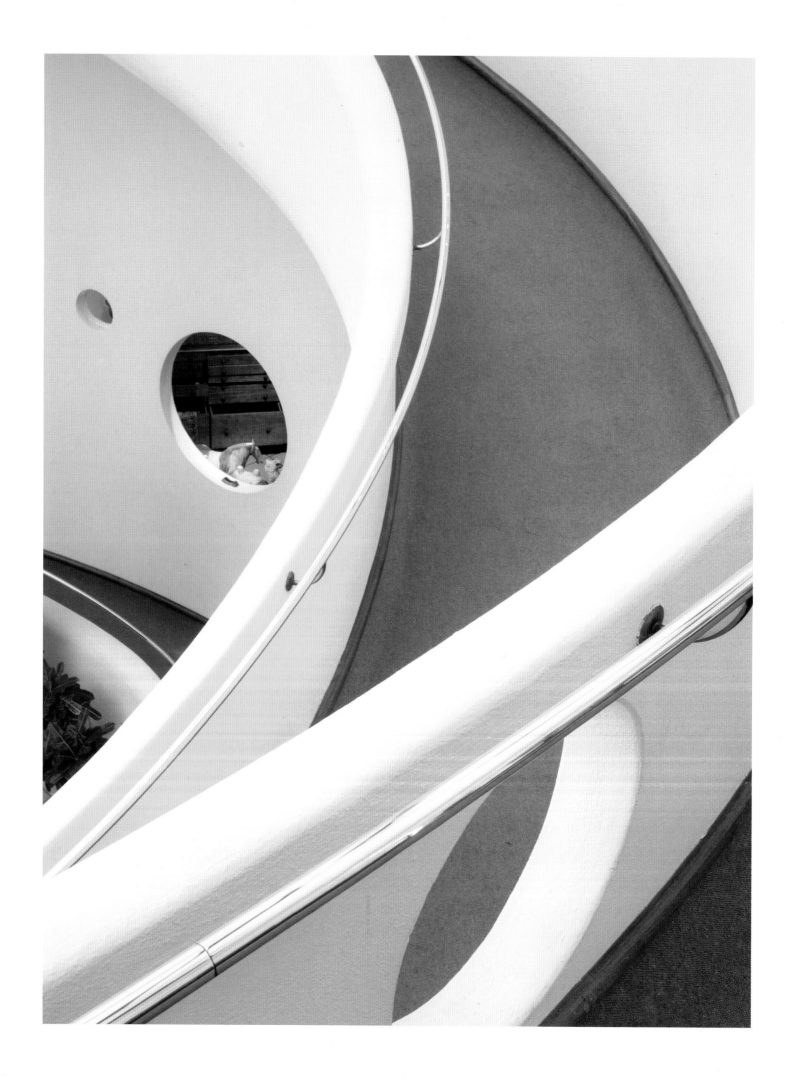

FRANK LLOYD WRIGHT
on the West Coast

Mark Anthony Wilson

photography by Joel Puliatti

GIBBS SMITH
TO ENRICH AND INSPIRE HUMANKIND

*This book is dedicated to my wife, Ann, and my daughter, Elena,
who are my greatest inspiration.*

First Edition
23 22   8 7 6 5

Published by
Gibbs Smith
P.O. Box 667
Layton, Utah 84041

1.800.835.4993 orders
www.gibbs-smith.com

Designed by Kurt Wahlner
Printed and bound in China

Gibbs Smith books are printed on paper produced from sustainable PEFC-
certified forest/controlled wood source. Learn more at www.pefc.org.

Library of Congress Cataloging-in-Publication Data

Wilson, Mark A. (Mark Anthony), author.
  Frank Lloyd Wright on the West Coast / Mark Anthony
Wilson ; photography by Joel Puliatti. — First Edition.
     pages cm
  Includes bibliographical references and index.
  ISBN 978-1-4236-3447-8
1. Wright, Frank Lloyd, 1867-1959—Themes, motives. 2. Architecture—
California—History—20th century. 3. Architecture—Oregon—History—20th
century. 4. Architecture—Washington (State)—History—20th century. I. Puliatti,
Joel, illustrator. II. Wright, Frank Lloyd, 1867-1959. Works. Selections. III. Title.
  NA737.W7W55 2014
  720.92—dc23
                2014000645

IMAGES—
CASE: Ablin House, east façade.

DOUBLE ENDSHEET, FRONT: Berger House, San
Anselmo, California (1950–58), floor plan. Copyright
© The Frank Lloyd Wright Foundation, Scottsdale,
Arizona.

SINGLE ENDSHEETS, FRONT AND BACK: Buehler House,
Orinda, California (1948–49), blueprint of north
and south elevations. Copyright © The Frank Lloyd
Wright Foundation, Scottsdale, Arizona.

DOUBLE ENDSHEET, BACK: Walton House, Modesto,
California (1957–61), blueprint of general plan.
Copyright © The Frank Lloyd Wright Foundation,
Scottsdale, Arizona.

FRONTISPIECE: V. C. Morris Gift Shop, San Francisco
(c. 1948–49), detail of spiral ramp.

CONTENTS

ACKNOWLEDGMENTS

First of all I want to thank my true friend and partner on this book, Joel Puliatti, whose superb photographs bring Frank Lloyd Wright's buildings to life in a way words by themselves could never do. His creative vision was an invaluable asset on this project. Next, I want to thank two people from the Frank Lloyd Wright Building Conservancy: Deborah Vick, who helped me with the initial contacts for many of the buildings in this book; and Larry Woodin, who showed us through Wright's houses in Washington, and provided critical input for the chapter on Wright's work in the Northwest.

Margo Stipe, archivist for the Frank Lloyd Wright Foundation, was very helpful in giving us permission to use some of Frank Lloyd Wright's blueprints and drawings, which grace several chapters in this book. Scot Zimmerman, photographer, was gracious in providing eight of his color photos for the book. Carol Acquaviva and Laurie Thompson at the Anne T. Kent California Room of the Marin County Free Library helped with my original research and obtaining archival images for the chapter on the Marin County Civic Center.

Crosby Doe, Realtor extraordinaire, was generous with his time in showing us through two of Wright's landmark homes featured in Chapter 4. Anthony Bruce of the Berkeley Architectural Heritage Association provided contact information for the owners of the Frank Lloyd Wright house in Berkeley. David Coffey, caretaker of the George Ablin House in Bakersfield, was also generous with his time, as was Bob Ray, executor of the Buehler Estate in Orinda. Renowned author

T. C. Boyle did more than let us spend several hours in his lovely Wright home in Santa Barbara County; he provided wonderful personal commentary on his house as well as on Wright himself. Jeffrey Herr, curator of the Hollyhock House, spent many hours providing information on the history of that site and its original owner, Aline Barnsdall. Also, Trudi Sandmeier, at the USC School of Architecture, arranged access to the Freeman House and provided several archival images for that section of the book. And Dorothy Knight, Konrad Pearce, Eric Berger, Chuck Henderson, Mark Griggs, Ann Corrin, Marsha Vargas Handley, and Vicky Tway all provided archival images and/or family photos from their Wright-designed buildings.

Molly Murphy, general director of the Gordon House in Oregon, provided much historical information, and an archival photo, for the section on that residence. Julie Cain, project coordinator for Stanford Heritage Services, was most generous in showing us through the Hanna House on the Stanford University campus as well as providing historical facts, and Daniel Hartwig at the Stanford University Archives helped me find archival images for that building.

Numerous friends gave their opinions and comments on various sections of this book. My thanks especially to Rheanna Bagley for her enthusiasm, input, and suggestions throughout this project. Tren Bender was also supportive during the early phases of this book. And of course the owners of the dozens of Frank Lloyd Wright buildings included in these pages have my sincere appreciation and gratitude for sharing their beautiful sites with me and

Millard House, Pasadena, California (1923–24), view from garden with guesthouse toward main house.

Joel, as well as providing interesting information about the history of their buildings.

My brother, John Wilson, provided valuable contact information for some of the Southern California sites. Tom Myers provided contact information and property profiles for several of the California houses. My editor at Gibbs Smith, Bob Cooper, was most helpful whenever I asked his opinion about certain aspects of my manuscript, and offered many suggestions for information that would enhance readers' understanding of Wright's work.

Finally, I want to thank my wife, Ann, and my daughter, Elena, for their patience and ideas throughout this project, and for their belief in me and this book. I quite literally could not have finished this endeavor without their loving support.

INTRODUCTION

"There also is a sort of style imported from the Middle West and consisting chiefly of plate glass and horizontal lines, which enjoys a wide vogue and a quite inexplicable reputation for originality."

—Horace G. Simpson, San Francisco architect, about Frank Lloyd Wright's influence, 1916

Most Americans with any interest in architecture are familiar with Frank Lloyd Wright's most famous buildings east of the Mississippi River. Wright's iconic structures, like the Robie House in Chicago (1909),[1] Fallingwater in western Pennsylvania (1936), and the Guggenheim Museum in New York City (1959), are included in almost every art history textbook that covers twentieth-century architecture. The high points of Wright's career have been publicized in a number of popular documentaries in recent years, such as Ken Burns's *Frank Lloyd Wright,* broadcast on PBS in 1998, and *The Homes of Frank Lloyd Wright,* shown on A&E in 1996. Scores of books have been published about Wright's architecture and his personal life since his death a few weeks before his 92nd birthday in 1959.

Yet comparatively few architecture buffs are familiar with Frank Lloyd Wright's West Coast buildings. With the notable exception of the Marin County Civic Center in San Rafael (1959), few people have seen images of Wright's work on the West Coast. Between 1909 and 1959, Wright designed and completed a total of 36 structures that were built on 28 sites up and down the West Coast, from Southern California to suburban Seattle. Thirty-four of these buildings remain intact in their original picturesque settings, with few if any alterations.

Wright's West Coast oeuvre includes lesser-known gems such as the George and Emily Stewart House in Santa Barbara County, a Prairie-style masterpiece built the same year as the Robie House; the Mrs. Clinton Walker House in Carmel (1948), which played a central role in the 1959 film *A Summer Place*; the Mayan-style

Charles Ennis House in Los Angeles (1923–24), used in the 1975 film *The Day of the Locust*; and the Anderton Court Shops, a Space Age–style shopping center in Beverly Hills (1952).

Wright created his own word to describe his California residential architecture: "Romanza." This term implied that his California residences were designed to blend in with their romantic settings in individual ways, taking into account the unique beauty of each site. These sites included the redwood- and live oak–covered hills in the San Francisco Bay Area, the scrub brush–crested dunes of Southern California deserts, the palm trees and lush flowers of the Hollywood Hills, the semitropical coastal vegetation of Santa Barbara, and the golden rolling hills of the Central Valley. In each of these sites, Wright used local building materials whenever feasible, in keeping with his emphasis on giving his architecture an organic quality, so that it seems to become a part of nature rather than trying to dominate it. These natural materials included pink Sonoma stone facing along exterior walls; polished redwood paneling in living rooms, dining rooms, and ceilings, as well as for framing doors and windows; stucco covering along exterior walls in Southern California; and yellow or red brick facing around entrances in Northern California.

In Oregon and Washington State, Wright designed a handful of little-known yet beautifully sited residences in the Usonian mode, his term for the simple modular type of housing he promoted as being adaptable to varied environments and affordable for the average middle-class family. His Usonian homes in the Northwest were all built in the 1950s, during the last decade of his

Frank Lloyd Wright at his drafting table at Taliesin West, c. 1958. Courtesy of Harold Stockstad Slide Collection, Anne T. Kent California Room, Marin County Free Library.

career. Most of Wright's California houses were also built in the Usonian style, between 1938 and 1958. This book also covers all of Wright's public and commercial buildings on the West Coast. Though few in number, their variety of styles, purposes, building materials, and sites make these structures just as interesting and worthy of attention as Wright's West Coast residential work.

Another aspect of Wright's career that has received scant attention in previous books is the debates he engaged in with several of his West Coast female clients, who were strong-willed and independent-minded enough to successfully lobby him to get major changes in his designs for their homes, despite Wright's reputation for being loath to make significant alterations to his residential plans for many previous clients. These stories are told in the chapters about Wright's

residential work in California during the 1940s and '50s, through letters between Wright and his clients, and with accounts of conversations they had with him. This book also tells the little-known story of how a remarkable woman named Vera Schultz, Marin County's first female supervisor, was able to prevail over an entrenched old boys' network to insist that Frank Lloyd Wright's controversial plans for their new civic center became a reality.

▼ ▼ ▼ ▼ ▼

My own interest in Frank Lloyd Wright's career began during my childhood. I grew up in Chicago's Hyde Park neighborhood in the 1950s and '60s. The tree-lined streets of this historic district,

Robie House, Chicago (1909), exterior and living room. Photographs by Mark A. Wilson.

which surrounds the University of Chicago campus, contain several of Wright's earliest residences, many of them prototypes for his Prairie School movement. In essence, Prairie School homes were the first modern houses. Wright's creation of this revolutionary design philosophy at the dawn of the twentieth century, in which he first applied his organic principles to make buildings blend in with their environment, forever changed the way residential architecture would look in the United States. His open, free-flowing floor plans, which he called "breaking the box," laid the groundwork for the classic ranch houses and midcentury modern homes that countless other architects would later design.

The most famous Prairie School residence was the Robie House, designed in 1906 and completed in 1909, located at 5757 South Woodlawn Avenue in Hyde Park. I often walked by this house on my way to school, and I would marvel at the difference between this futuristic-looking home and all the other ornate, Edwardian-era houses around it that were built at the same time. The Robie House is considered to be so important to the history of twentieth-century architecture that it is one of the few single-family residences nominated for the United Nations' UNESCO

World Heritage List, (Wright's Fallingwater house in western Pennsylvania has also been nominated, as well as the Marin County Civic Center and Hollyhock House in California).[2]

Wright's radical new ideas were not readily accepted by the established architects and critics of his day. Many architectural firms in the United States, particularly on the West Coast, continued to design homes in the various popular Period Revival modes well into the twentieth century. Horace G. Simpson, who had a successful San Francisco firm and was a staunch advocate of the Tudor Revival style for his wealthy clients, wrote a harsh condemnation of the Prairie School movement in the February 1916 issue of *The Architect and Engineer of California*:

> *There also is a sort of style imported from the Middle West and consisting chiefly of plate glass and horizontal lines, which enjoys a wide vogue and a quite inexplicable reputation for originality. Without doubt our domestic architecture is suffering from the taint of egotism in the designers which causes them to express their own peculiarities rather than the uses of the building and the personality of its occupants.*[3]

BELOW: Hollyhock House, Los Angeles (1917–21), view of parapets. RIGHT: Marin County Civic Center, San Rafael, California (1959–62), Administration Building.

Such pompous criticism did not deter Wright or his followers in spreading the innovative design concepts of the Prairie School across the Unites States. This included the West Coast, where Prairie-style homes were being designed by a new generation of architects for avant-garde clients by the early 1910s. These radical ideas of what good residential design should look like were propelled in large part by Wright's supreme sense of confidence in his own abilities. At the tender age of 21, he had been hired as a draftsman by the leading midwestern architectural firm of Adler & Sullivan. After becoming head draftsman and getting his own office there by the age of 24, Wright began independently designing homes for some of Sullivan's best clients. When Sullivan found out about this "moonlighting," he reacted angrily and fired Wright.[4] So in 1893, at the age of 26, Wright opened his own practice out of his home studio in suburban Oak Park, Illinois. This event was a watershed in American architectural history, since Wright's career blossomed after that, bringing him international fame within the next decade, while Sullivan suffered a steady decline in his clientele from that year forward. By the end of his career 66 years later, Wright had designed a total of 1,141 projects, of which 532 were built during his lifetime, and 410 still stand.[5]

Ennis House, Los Angeles (1923–24).

▼ ▼ ▼ ▼ ▼

To say that Wright's ideas, as well as some of his public statements, were controversial would be a major understatement. His ego was legendary, matched only by his indomitable will. These qualities served him well in the struggles he endured to gain public and official approval for two of his most famous projects: the Guggenheim Museum in New York City and the Marin County Civic Center.

The first one was the last public project he supervised before his death, and the second one was the only one of his government projects ever built. Wright's reaction to some of his critics during the planning of the Marin County Civic Center is revealed in Chapter 7. His often sarcastic nature and his unbridled arrogance, which he made no effort to hide, are clearly illustrated by three anecdotes that were related to me by firsthand witnesses.

In 1957, my parents attended a lecture given by Frank Lloyd Wright at the University of Chicago, which was open to the public as well as university students. The talk was followed by a question-and-answer session. Before the lecture began, my father overheard two students discussing how they planned to "stump the master" by asking Wright a question he would have trouble answering, and if he didn't give a straight answer to the first student, the second one would stand up immediately and demand he answer the previous question. When Wright had concluded his lecture and asked if there were any questions, the first student raised his hand and Wright acknowledged him. He stood up with a slight smirk on his face and said, "Mr. Wright, you have always said that good architecture should not include any features that are not useful or functional—correct?" Wright nodded in agreement. "Well, in your design for the Herbert Johnson House in

Wisconsin, you included a staircase alongside the fireplace that leads nowhere—it just ends with an empty platform that has no door or window behind it. How do you explain this contradiction of your own principles?" The student sat down with a smug smile on his face. A murmur of surprise rippled through the audience. Wright paused, cleared his throat, and said, "Next question." The second student stood up and demanded, "Mr. Wright, I'd like you to answer that last question, please!" Wright's eyes narrowed slightly, and then he gave a classic Wright comeback. "All right, you want to know why I included that staircase, so I'll tell you. I designed it so that the two of you could climb up to the top—and jump off! Next question."[6]

In one of the classes I taught on American architecture at Vista Community College (now Berkeley City College) in the early 1980s, there was a student whose mother had been one of Wright's secretaries at Taliesin West, his studio near Scottsdale, Arizona, in the early 1940s. She told my class about one of her most vivid memories of Wright, recalling a brief conversation she had with him. One afternoon when she was about 12 years old, she was sitting on the floor of Wright's drafting room reading a book of Bible stories to pass the time while her mother worked on some of Wright's papers at her desk nearby. Wright himself was busy working on some drawings at his drafting table a few feet from her. Suddenly it occurred to her to ask Wright a question born out of innocent childhood curiosity. So she walked over to his drafting table and stood next to it until she got his attention. After a few seconds Wright looked up at her and smiled. "Yes, what's on your mind, child?" he asked.

"Mr. Wright, do you ever read the Bible?"

"Yes, I've read parts of it on occasion."

"Well, do you believe in God then?"

"Why yes, I do. I have to believe in him—since God and I have something in common, after all."

"And what is that?" she asked in a puzzled voice.

"*He* was a creator too."[7]

During the public debate over final approval of Wright's design for the Marin County Civic Center, he was attacked by some county officials and the local chapter of the VFW as being unpatriotic and a "Communist sympathizer." These types of accusations had been directed against him even by his neighbors in Spring Green, Wisconsin, where he had his Taliesin East studio. One resident who remembers such innuendos is Margaret Lins Stewart, whose father, Albert Lins, worked as a handyman at Taliesin East in the late 1930s and early 1940s. She recalled that many of the residents in town were vocal about their dislike of Wright, saying that he must be running "some type of Communist commune" at Taliesin East, because everyone there had to share all the tasks and ate common meals. They also resented the fact that Wright was exempt from paying any taxes on this property because it was given an exemption as a "school" instead of a farm.[8]

Much like Pablo Picasso, another seminal artist of the twentieth century whose work forever changed the nature of his medium, Frank Lloyd Wright's work as an architect should be viewed separately from his personality and his private life. Neither man was a paragon of virtuous behavior when it came to how they treated some of the women in their lives, and both men had enormous egos and often spoke and acted arrogantly in public. Yet no objective observer can deny that their innovative techniques and original ideas altered the way we look at the world, and blazed trails for future generations of practitioners in their respective design fields that are still being followed. Today, Frank Lloyd Wright is not only considered to be the greatest American architect of all time,[9] but one of the most influential architects in history. A genius like Wright only comes along once every few generations. The 1970 song "So Long, Frank Lloyd Wright" by Simon and Garfunkel, which eloquently expressed the debt we owe to his creative genius, is but one example of how his legacy left its mark on our popular culture.

This book is intended for those who want to better understand Frank Lloyd Wright's contributions to the quality of the built environment on the West Coast. I hope you enjoy the journey.

—Mark Anthony Wilson
Berkeley, California
February 2014

CHAPTER 1
A PRAIRIE AMONG THE PALMS
The Stewart House, Santa Barbara County, 1909

"I see him as one of the original hippies, a touchstone figure who brought us out from behind the walls of closed-in rooms and back into the embrace of nature."

— T. C. Boyle, author, on Frank Lloyd Wright's legacy, 2013

By 1909, at the age of 42, Frank Lloyd Wright had earned a solid reputation as America's most innovative architect. During his 16 years of private practice he had created an impressive body of work in dozens of cities across the Midwest and the Northeast, and his articles and essays on architectural theory had gained the respect of architects and critics on both sides of the Atlantic. His design for the Prairie-style Robie House in Chicago three years earlier was hailed as the prototype for twentieth-century residences. Yet in the fall of that year, Wright risked everything he had achieved by running off to Europe with Mamah Cheney, the wife of one of his clients, leaving behind his wife and six children. But shortly before he left, he completed the design for his first building on the West Coast, the George and Emily Stewart House in Santa Barbara County. This house remains standing today nearly as he designed it, and is one of only two examples of Wright's Prairie-style houses ever built on the West Coast (the other is on the grounds of Hollyhock House in Los Angeles).

The Stewart House is located in Montecito, a forested, upscale enclave adjacent to the southern city limits of Santa Barbara. It was a small, rural community in 1909, when it was known to locals as "the fashionable neighborhood of Santa Barbara."[1] Today it boasts many impressive residences by such distinguished twentieth-century architects as Bernard Maybeck, Gardner Dailey, Richard Neutra, and George Washington Smith. At that time, the city of Santa Barbara was already famous for its historic Spanish Colonial town center

and the clusters of towering palm trees along its coastline. The city was experiencing a major boom in the early years of the twentieth century, as people built both primary residences and vacation homes there. The population of the city nearly doubled between 1900 and 1910, growing from 6,587 to nearly 12,000 residents.[2]

George Stewart was a Scottish immigrant who worked as an accountant in Seattle before moving to Fresno, where his family owned orchards and a vineyard. In 1909 he decided he wanted to build a vacation home near the coast, and chose a five-acre lot in Montecito to build it on. His wife, Emily, wrote to Frank Lloyd Wright about designing their getaway home, after seeing articles about his Prairie-style homes in several magazines. He agreed to design for them a "summer cottage," as his plans would be labeled, since he needed money for his then secret plan to move to Europe with his mistress, Mamah Cheney.[3] Wright never visited the site, since he was preoccupied with preparations for his trip at that time. Nonetheless, he produced a complete set of working drawings, which included a gardener's cottage, stables, and a work shed. Wright considered his design for the Stewart House to be important enough to include a large perspective drawing of it in his Wasmuth portfolio, the collection of his plans and drawings that he and Mamah Cheney brought with them to Europe, to be published in Germany as a book about his work. The Stewarts would alter Wright's plans a bit, by enclosing an open-air porch on the west end of the ground floor before moving in, and by extending the first-floor bedroom wing and adding a half bath in 1930. They also constructed a guesthouse at the rear of the lot in the 1920s.[4]

FACING: Stewart House, Santa Barbara County (1909).

Stewart House, east façade.

The Stewarts nicknamed their vacation home "Butterfly Woods," because of the thousands of monarch butterflies that used to swarm this area of Montecito every fall. The entrance to their house was originally on the eastern side, off Butterfly Lane. Several years later the entrance was moved to its current location on the north side. The heavily wooded lot has eucalyptus, pine, and tea trees, and thick bushes that shade the house and shelter it from the neighboring homes on the east, west, and south sides. The house is set well back from the street behind a wide lawn on the north side. Wright sited the house between two giant pine trees, which died several years ago, and he placed a carriage house below the original entrance, which was converted into a house and sold when the lot was divided. The current 1.1-acre lot still has a very exotic and romantic ambience, with its thick semitropical vegetation, including a variety of ferns, century-old tea trees, and towering eucalyptus trees. The house was constructed of redwood framing, with horizontal board-and-batten paneling along the exterior, which adds to the feeling of its being part of nature. The low-angled hipped roofline differs from most of Wright's Prairie houses back east, where the roofs were usually flat. However, the wide overhanging eaves and the horizontal massing of this two-story residence are classic Prairie elements. The floor plan of this house is a cruciform, which was unusual for Wright's California residences. Construction was completed in 1910.

▼ ▼ ▼ ▼ ▼

Upon entering the Stewart House, Wright's classic technique of using low ceilings that open into a grand space (or "compression and release," as he called it) is immediately apparent. A six-and-a-half-foot-tall ceiling just inside the doorway rises to a breathtaking twenty-foot-high cathedral ceiling in the two-story living room. A tall, brick-faced fireplace dominates the west wall. An overhanging balcony above the fireplace runs the length of the west wall, providing a view over the living room from the second floor.

Wright placed the other two public rooms on the north and west ends, flanking the living room and creating a pleasing sense of symmetry. To the left is the formal dining room, and to the right is the library. In both of these rooms, Wright placed a six-and-a-half-foot ceiling at the entry, and then raised the ceilings to a height of about eight and a half feet, and lined them with pent redwood beams. There is a short rise of steps up into the living room from these two rooms, which creates a sense of dramatic change as you walk into the much grander space.

All three of the public rooms are flooded with natural light from rows of banded windows that line every exterior wall.

Stewart House, second-floor plan. Copyright © The Frank Lloyd Wright Foundation, Scottsdale, Arizona.

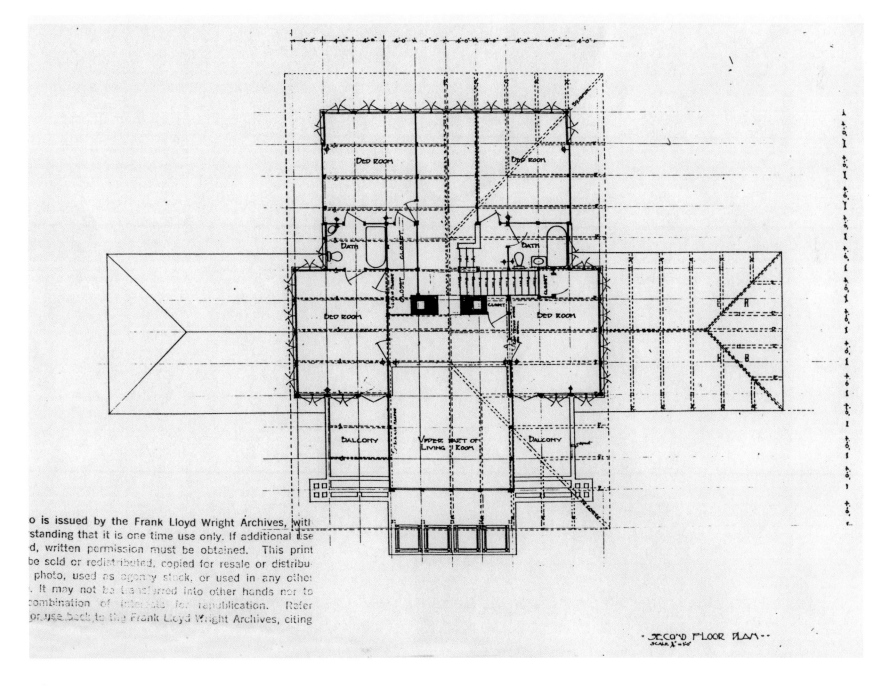

These elegant, redwood-framed casement windows all have an Arts and Crafts T-shaped decorative motif, which symbolizes the tea trees on the lot. The views from each of the three public rooms are of the sylvan surroundings, creating a serene, peaceful ambience, and enhancing the indoor-outdoor effect that Wright intended with all his Prairie-style residences. There are a total of 365 of these windows throughout the house, and they are all original. These windows still have all their original metal

LEFT: Stewart House, living room. ABOVE: Stewart House, living room fireplace.

latches, and they open outward. The floors in the three downstairs public rooms are oak. The library has built-in bookshelves, and both it and the dining room have projecting bays in the center of their far walls.

Adjacent to the dining room, in the west wing, are the pantry and kitchen, easily accessible through a wide door. The rest of this wing has two bedrooms and one and a half baths. A wide hallway leads down the middle of the west wing to the porch the Stewarts enclosed, which they used as a powder room and is now a sitting room. Wright included a partial basement, another unusual feature for his California homes. It was originally intended to be used

Stewart House, view from living room into dining room.

Stewart House, dining room.

Stewart House, library.

as a garage, but ended up being used as space for a laundry room, workshop, and darkroom.

Upstairs there are three bedrooms and two baths off the central hallway, including the master suite. Another glass-enclosed porch runs along the entire west end of this wing. At the northeast corner of the second floor is a small open-air deck beneath the wide overhanging eaves, which could be used as a sleeping porch, a common feature in multistory early twentieth-century homes. The attic still houses the original 1,000-gallon water storage tank, the base of which is an extension of the chimney flue. This is a version of the central utility core, which Wright pioneered with the Robie House in Chicago, and used on many of his multistory houses after that.

The elegant living room fireplace is characteristic of many of Wright's earlier Prairie houses back east. It is faced with red brick, and has a simple Arts and Crafts–style wooden shelf mantel. Built-in, glass-fronted bookcases on either side of the fireplace were designed by Stickley and commissioned and installed by the current owners. The Arts and Crafts–style copper-and-tinted-glass hanging light fixture in the living room is original, and it displays the same classic right angles found on the light fixtures in most of Wright's other Prairie houses. Most of the copper wall sconces throughout the house are original, and were designed by Wright.

The Stewarts occupied this house for 33 years, until 1942. Then Greta Blickenstaff bought it and lived there for 42 years, until 1984. After a brief tenure by a third owner, Jerald Peterson bought it. He did some cleanup of the grounds and some renovations to the interior of the house, then put the house on the market.[5]

In 1993, acclaimed novelist and short story writer T. C. Boyle bought the house, and he and his wife, Karen, have lived there ever since. In 2009, T. C. Boyle published a novel titled *The Women,* which is about Frank Lloyd Wright's relationship with his three wives and his mistress, Mamah Cheney. Boyle was inspired to write this book by having raised his family in the Wright-designed Stewart House. "I wrote *The Women* as a way of informing myself about the architect who designed the house I was living in, and restoring. I see him as one of the original hippies, a touchstone figure who brought us out from behind the walls of closed-in rooms and back into the embrace of nature. Of course, I do suspect that he may have been a wee bit full of himself. Was this healthy ego justified in his work? A thousand times over. What does it matter when it is the work that lives on?"[6]

When they moved in, all of the interior woodwork had been painted white by a previous owner. So T. C. and his wife stripped all the woodwork in the three public rooms on the ground floor. The foundation of the house was on piers that were not earthquake safe. So they put in a new foundation built of poured concrete, and had the house earthquake retrofitted. They also replaced the old shake roof with one of composite shingles that had the appearance of the original roof. Boyle also did extensive landscape work on the lot, including creating water features for the yard, building privacy fences, and constructing a parking pad and wooden cover near the west end of the property.

Boyle's children are now all grown and moved out, but he told me this house was the perfect place to raise a family. "This is a very livable house. We raised three children here and there was plenty of room for everybody. We were the first family that had lived here since the 1940s, but we rediscovered the fact that this really is a family house."[7]

Boyle described to me his first impression of the Stewart House, and what made him want to live in it. "It was my wife who first found the house. She called me from Santa Barbara (we were living in L.A. then) and began sobbing over the phone because she loved the house so much and was afraid I wouldn't. We both came up the following day and immediately bought the place. My first view of it was of the north side of the house, and then I was led in through the doorway on that side, under the amazing cantilevers and into the two-story atrium room, where the Realtor, Bill Sloniker, was standing before the fireplace. Bill, who subsequently became a close friend, was an expert on Wright and especially on the Stewart House. He provided a running commentary as we walked through the rooms, and the enormous charm and utility of the place began to astonish me all over again. It still astonishes me, all these many years later."[8]

With his design for the George Stewart House in 1909, Frank Lloyd Wright completed his first California commission, the first of two dozen that would be built in the Golden State over the next 50 years. He would not receive a second California commission for eight more years, when he was hired to design the Aline Barnsdall House in 1917 in Los Angeles (see Chapter 2). Yet Wright's West Coast legacy would be substantial, since he developed several new construction techniques and design concepts for his West Coast clients. These ideas would inspire a new generation of architects, and influence homebuilding throughout the United States for decades to come.

Below: Stewart House, south façade. Facing: Stewart House, exterior detail.

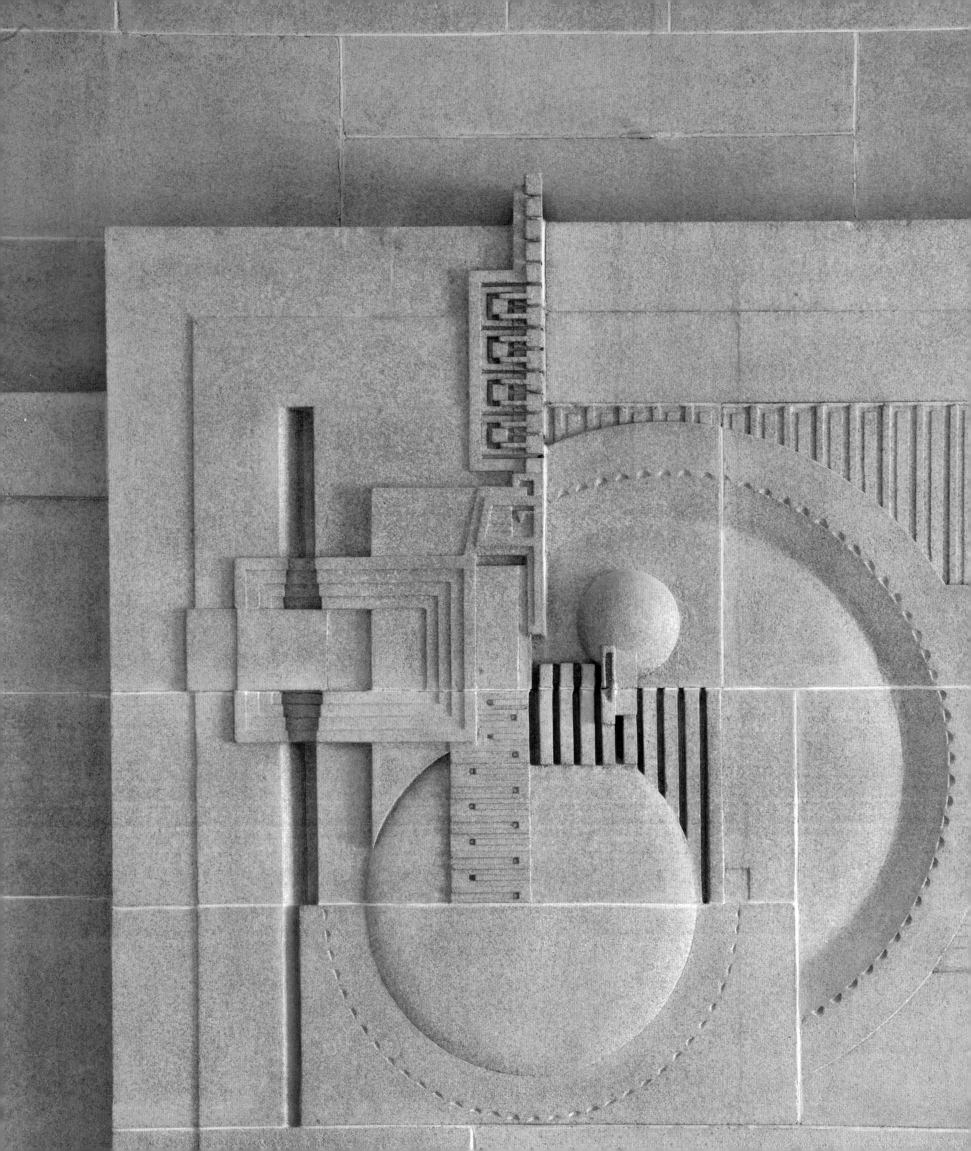

CHAPTER 2
A MAYAN TEMPLE IN HOLLYWOOD
The Barnsdall (Hollyhock) House, Los Angeles, 1917–21

"Its use of indoor/outdoor spaces marks it as a prototype of the modern ranch house."

— Jeffrey Herr, curator of the Hollyhock House, 2013

The Hollywood Hills were still mostly open grassland in 1919, the year Los Angeles oil heiress Aline Barnsdall bought a 36-acre tract called Olive Hill on a hilltop above Hollywood Boulevard, just west of Vermont Avenue. The village of Hollywood had been incorporated into the city of Los Angeles in 1910, and the first movie to be filmed there by D. W. Griffith, working for the Biograph Company, had begun production that same year. But the hills remained largely undeveloped, until the first major hillside residential tract was laid out in 1918.[1]

Aline Barnsdall was a patroness of the arts, and she had a special passion for the theater. Her dream was to build a performing arts complex that would include a state-of-the-art theater, a residence for herself and her daughter, apartments for actors, and eventually commercial shops, artists' studios, and a motion picture theater. Barnsdall chose Frank Lloyd Wright as the architect for this project, both because of his reputation as a progressive designer and his love for the arts.[2] In the end, only four structures were actually built, three of which remain standing—and are now part of Barnsdall Art Park, owned by the city of Los Angeles.

Aline Barnsdall was an unusual woman in several ways. She had inherited a large fortune from her father, yet she was an outspoken supporter of the Russian Revolution from its beginning. Aline also had a close friendship with the famous American anarchist Emma Goldman. She chose to never marry, but gave birth

to a daughter by a live-in lover. After living in Europe during her teenage years, she moved to Chicago before World War I and became a patron of the avant-garde Little Theater, which staged productions of controversial new plays.[3]

Barnsdall first approached Frank Lloyd Wright in Chicago in 1915 about designing a new facility for the Little Theater. She soon changed her mind, and decided to build her own theater in Los Angeles, which had a thriving theater scene by the 1910s in

FACING: Hollyhock House, Los Angeles (1917–21), detail of living room fireplace mantel. RIGHT: Aline Barnsdall and her daughter, Betty, 1922. Courtesy of Mark Wanamaker, Bison Archives.

addition to its growing fame as a home for the new motion picture industry.[4] Between 1910 and 1920, the population of Los Angeles grew from about 300,000 to nearly 600,000, and the city was attracting talented young professionals and artists from all over the United States.[5]

In addition to patrons of the arts like Aline Barnsdall, the booming economy of Los Angeles convinced both Frank Lloyd Wright's daughter Catherine and his eldest son, Lloyd, to make their homes there in the 1910s. Lloyd opened his own successful architecture practice in Los Angeles in 1915, and he and his father would collaborate on several residential commissions there over the next decade, including the home that his father would design for Aline Barnsdall. Under the influence of his children and the ongoing multiyear commission for Barnsdall, Wright would move his office to Los Angeles in 1923, and stay there for the next two years. After living in Southern California, Wright was famously

quoted as saying, "Tip the world over on its side and everything loose will land in Los Angeles."[6] Nevertheless, his personal dedication to completing the seven residences he designed in the city of Los Angeles over a 20-year period—including the three on Olive Hill—belies that sentiment.

At the time Wright first met Aline Barnsdall, he had begun incorporating elements of pre-Columbian motifs into some of his designs, especially ones from Mayan temples in the jungles of Central America. Wright had been intrigued with pre-Columbian architecture since he was in his 20s, when he had seen ersatz examples of such buildings at the World's Columbian Exposition in Chicago in 1893. He had used some of these motifs on his design for the warehouse for A. D. German in Richland Center, Wisconsin, in 1915. The upper portion of the walls on this warehouse clearly display massing and geometric decorations that were borrowed from temples in Chichen Itza, on the Yucatan Peninsula.[7] That same year

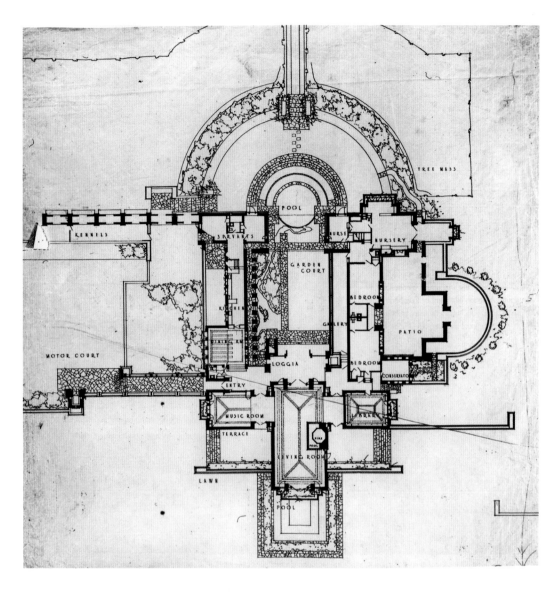

FACING: Hollyhock House, west façade. RIGHT: Hollyhock House, floor plan. Copyright © The Frank Lloyd Wright Foundation, Scottsdale, Arizona.

Wright designed the Imperial Hotel in Tokyo, which also had pre-Columbian elements, such as its heavy masonry walls and geometric ornaments around the main entrance.

Wright's first drawings for the Barnsdall House in 1917 included three different styles: a Prairie house, a modified neo-Gothic house, and a blend of sweeping horizontal Prairie lines with pre-Columbian-type massing and decorative motifs. The last version would be close to the final design of the house as it was eventually built. But the journey from these preliminary drawings to the actual construction of the buildings on Olive Hill would be a long and difficult one, filled with construction challenges, communication problems, and design changes that would test both the working relationship and friendship between Wright and his mercurial client.

The lot Barnsdall purchased in the Hollywood Hills was a problematic site for such a grand project. The top of Olive Hill was barren and dusty, although it did provide unimpeded views of downtown Los Angeles to the south, the San Gabriel Mountains to the north, and the Pacific Ocean to the west. However, it was far from the commercial center of Los Angeles, and quite isolated from the settled part of Hollywood. Overall it had very little to offer any serious developer, unless they had a unique vision and an unrelenting passion for seeing a dream realized, as Jeffrey Herr, curator of Hollyhock House, points out in his 2005 monograph on the history of Olive Hill.[8] (The nickname "Hollyhock House" was derived from the stylized hollyhock motifs Wright designed for the concrete finials on the exterior of the house. Hollyhocks were Aline Barnsdall's favorite flower, and they were growing in abundance on Olive Hill when she purchased the property.)

The period between 1915, when Frank Lloyd Wright first discussed the theater project with Barnsdall, and 1924, when Barnsdall finally gave up on her dream of completing her grand development, was a particularly difficult phase in Wright's

Hollyhock House, detail of west façade.

professional and personal life. In August 1914 he lost both his lover Mamah Cheney and Taliesin, his home and studio in Wisconsin, in a horrific fire and multiple murder. Cheney, her two children, and four of Wright's apprentices were killed by a deranged house servant named Julian Carlton at Taliesin while Wright was away giving a lecture in Milwaukee. Carlton killed his victims with a hatchet, after setting the house on fire. Then, early in 1915, Wright began a romance with a divorcée named Miriam Noel while he was still legally married to his first wife, Catherine. He would eventually marry Miriam, but it would be a volatile, on-again, off-again relationship, one in which private letters from Miriam to Wright, written in anger during one of their separations, would be published in several major newspapers. Wright married her in late 1923, but she left him for good six months later. A bitter divorce followed, which led to more salacious press coverage.

All of the public scrutiny Wright received from these various scandals distracted him from his work, and undoubtedly made some potential clients shy away from hiring him. Wright was also being described by some critics at this time as out of touch with the new minimalist International style coming out of Europe, and an architect whose work was hopelessly romantic and outdated. The upshot was that during the time he was working actively with Aline Barnsdall, from 1918 through 1921, he had no other American commissions, which inevitably caused constant cash flow problems.

Hollyhock House, full view of living room fireplace.

Hollyhock House, detail of living room doorway.

Wright did, however, have a number of important commissions in Japan, which would include several private residences, a girls' school, and the Imperial Hotel and annex. These projects kept him in Japan for months at a time during the years he worked on the Olive Hill designs, thus delaying and complicating communications between him and Barnsdall. Her frequent design changes and reimagining of the project scope were another source of tension between the client and architect. An additional cause of stress in their working relationship was the strict budgetary limits that Barnsdall imposed on the project that she expected Wright to adhere to, something Wright was never good at doing. Finally, the headstrong, ego-driven personalities of Wright and Barnsdall led to constant clashes over design issues, and eventually ill will between them.

Construction on the Barnsdall House, or Hollyhock House, began in 1919, after Barnsdall had decided she needed to have a comfortable residence for herself and her daughter before work could begin on her theater and commercial buildings. She chose to put her residence at the top of Olive Hill, which provided the most spectacular views of the Los Angeles Basin and the nearby mountains. But this required significant design changes from Wright, who had previously been working under the assumption that the theater was to be the building that would be placed on the crown of the hill. Due to his spending so much time in Japan working on the Imperial Hotel annex in Tokyo, Wright chose his son Lloyd to be

Hollyhock House, east façade.

the supervising architect for the construction of Hollyhock House.

The house was constructed of hollow clay tiles covered by stucco, over a balloon frame construction. The ornamental hollyhock finials along the upper walls are made of cast concrete. The use of hollow clay tiles for load-bearing walls was an experimental technique at that time. Two years later, Wright employed one of his first uses of textile blocks (i.e., precast concrete blocks) for exterior walls on his plans for the schoolhouse he designed for Barnsdall on Olive Hill.

Hollyhock House is a two-story, 6,000-square-foot, T-shaped residence, with 16 rooms: seven bedrooms, including two servants' bedrooms; seven baths; a large living room; a formal dining room; a music room; a library; a conservatory; and an enclosed sun porch. Wright arranged the living room, which is on the western side behind an entrance loggia, at a right angle to the flanking music room and library. The other main rooms (the kitchen, dining room, and bedrooms) are grouped around a central open "garden court," as it is labeled on his plans. There is another walled patio off the south end of the house, and there is a small reflecting pool in front of the west entrance and a children's wading pool with terraced seating surrounding it at the eastern end. Both these pools are made of cast concrete. Wright also designed a nearby pergola, and had a row of kennels running off the northeast corner of the house. All of these features survive today just as he designed them.

The entrance to the house provides another classic example of Wright's compression-and-release technique: visitors enter through a low-ceilinged entry hall into the soaring space of the living room. The living room is dominated by a massive chimney made of concrete blocks along the south wall. The chimney rises up through the high ceiling, which is raised an extra two feet at the corners of the wide flue to maximize its visual impact. There is a large skylight over the fireplace, with a geometric pattern of wood framing. The overmantel is decorated with an intricate incised design of interlocking circles and triangles reminiscent of a Kandinsky painting. Wright placed a small concrete pool in the floor in front of the fireplace, to reflect the light from the flames at night. During a subsequent restoration, this pool was filled in with a concrete slab pad. It is now back to its original appearance, without the water in the pool.

Another outstanding feature Wright incorporated into his design for the Barnsdall House was the use of rhythmic geometric patterns in lead on many of the casement windows on bay windows and in hallways. On the wide squared bay in the nursery room, for instance, the wood-frame banded windows have zigzag and chevron patterns that are several years ahead of their time in their Art Deco–like geometric lines. The Art Deco movement began in Europe in the mid-1920s, after the discovery of King Tut's tomb created a mania for motifs from exotic ancient cultures, while Hollyhock House was completed in 1921.

Wright's innovative use of such geometric patterns can also be seen on the concrete finials with stylized hollyhock motifs that give a distinctly Art Deco–like appearance to the outer walls all around the house. The contrasting color scheme Wright chose for the exterior walls was also quite unusual for the times. The cast concrete finials were a tawny golden hue, and the walls were painted a silvery green, according to a contemporary newspaper account.[9] (However, Jeffrey Herr says that evidence from the recent restoration indicates all the cast concrete had a smooth gray look.[10]) During subsequent restorations, these colors were changed, but the current restoration project will restore the original color scheme.

▼ ▼ ▼ ▼ ▼

While Aline Barnsdall's residence was still under construction, she asked Wright to design two guesthouses on Olive Hill in 1920. These structures were called Residence A and Residence B, and they were finished about the same time as the main house. Wright

had still not completed a working set of drawings for the theater that Barnsdall so passionately wanted. Yet despite her disappointment over this fact, she asked him to also design a private schoolhouse for her daughter and other children, down the hill a little way from Hollyhock House, in 1923. So Wright rented Residence B for a while during the early phase of this project. Before the schoolhouse foundation could be completed, inspectors from the City of Los Angeles halted the construction for alleged code violations. Wright never finished the schoolhouse; its foundation was used by Austrian-born architect Rudolph Schindler to design an open-air play space, now called Schindler's Terrace. Meanwhile, Wright had the interior of Residence B remodeled for use as his studio, and went over the $30,000 budget limit that Barnsdall had set, further aggravating the tensions between them.[11] Residence B was demolished in 1948, but Residence A still stands near the east side of the Barnsdall House. It is a classic example of Wright's stuccoed Prairie-style houses, and the only one still standing on the West Coast (although it was suffering from years of deferred maintenance at this writing). With its wide overhanging eaves, flat roof, clean stucco walls, banded plate glass windows, horizontal massing, and refined geometric patterns on the narrow friezes above and below the windows, it resembles many of Wright's earlier Prairie-style homes throughout the Midwest.

The various disappointments that Aline Barnsdall experienced during the construction phase of her Olive Hill project, including building delays, cost overruns, and Wright's failure to produce a complete set of working drawings for the theater, caused a marked deterioration in their relationship by the early 1920s. Indeed, she fired him from the project temporarily in 1921, then rehired him to remodel Residence B and design the nearby schoolhouse. After construction on the school was halted, she fired him once again, and he threatened to sue her for unpaid bills related to the construction costs for Hollyhock House.[12] These issues were eventually settled out of court, but the constant tensions between them had taken their toll.

In addition to these problems, Barnsdall never really liked living in the house Wright designed for her. The second floor remained unfinished for years, and the roof leaked almost immediately. So she only spent brief periods of time in the house. By 1924 she had lost all her enthusiasm for the project. She decided to give the residence, the two guesthouses, and 11 acres of land on the crown of Olive Hill to the City of Los Angeles. But the unfinished state of the buildings and the deed restrictions she insisted on caused the city to reject her offer. So she hired Rudolph Schindler to finish the upstairs of Hollyhock House, and complete the schoolhouse and the remodeling of Residence B. She also hired Lloyd Wright to complete the landscaping.

When this work was finished, she offered the four buildings and the 11 acres of land to the city once again, and her offer was finally accepted in 1927.[13] As for Barnsdall, she and Wright did

point, FEMA became involved in the restoration and retrofitting of the structures, but their budget wasn't sufficient to complete such a large and complex project. So additional funding from both the State of California and the City of Los Angeles was secured. Hollyhock House was reopened to the public in 2005.[15] However, it soon became clear that the main residence needed a thorough restoration, due to recurring water damage. Thus a new preservation project began in 2010 under the direction of Jeffrey Herr, and is scheduled to be completed in 2014.

Commenting to me on the importance of Hollyhock House in American architectural history and its place in Wright's legacy,

Left: Barnsdall Estate, Residence A (1920). Facing: Hollyhock House, detail of finials.

eventually reconcile and renewed their friendship, although they never worked together again. Curiously, she did ask Wright a few years later to design a residence for her in Beverly Hills, but that proposal never got past the initial drawing stage. Aline Barnsdall spent the last few years of her life living part-time in Residence B, and she died alone in her bedroom there in 1946.[14]

▼ ▼ ▼ ▼

The 1994 Northridge earthquake did extensive damage to the buildings on Olive Hill, especially Hollyhock House. At that

Herr summed it up this way: "This was Wright's first residence in greater Los Angeles, and the first residence of his later period. It influenced not only his later work, but also that of R. M. Schindler and Richard Neutra. And its use of indoor/outdoor spaces marks it as a prototype of the modern ranch house."[16] Although Aline Barnsdall may not have achieved her ultimate dream of a center for performing arts, her vision did lead to the creation of one of America's most innovative and influential houses.

CHAPTER 3
PRE-COLUMBIAN MONUMENTS IN CONCRETE
Four Southern California Houses, 1923–25

"I would rather have built this little house than St. Peter's in Rome."
— Frank Lloyd Wright, about the Millard House, 1925

Concrete was a material that Frank Lloyd Wright began experimenting with in the early 1900s. His first use of reinforced concrete as a building material was on the Unity Temple in Oak Park, Illinois, designed in 1904. This landmark structure had unadorned reinforced concrete walls and roofs. Though this was not the first use of reinforced concrete for a tall building in the United States (the Ponce de Leon Hotel in St. Augustine, Florida, designed in 1886, was the first), Wright touted the versatility of this material after the Unity Temple, and helped popularize its use for a wide variety of buildings throughout America. He especially liked concrete's plasticity, or the ease with which it could be molded into various forms without losing its strength.

By the early 1920s, when Wright was living in Los Angeles, he began to experiment with a new adaptation of concrete as a building material for the walls of a house. He called this system "textile blocks," which were essentially two parallel rows of 12-inch-thick square concrete blocks, with an air pocket between them. Steel reinforcing rods were inserted between the blocks at even intervals to tie the blocks together and stabilize the walls. There is some question as to who deserves the credit for inventing this system (one of Wright's former assistants, Walter Burley Griffin, developed a similar concrete block system of building around the same time).[1] But Wright was the first architect to use this new system on a large scale for residences. He designed four houses

in Los Angeles County in the 1920s that were built out of textile blocks. All four of these homes remain standing today, and they have retained almost all of their original features.

The first textile block house Frank Lloyd Wright designed was the Alice Millard House, at 645 Prospect Crescent in Pasadena. Alice Millard was an importer and dealer in antique furnishings and rare books. In 1906, she and her husband, George, had Wright design a wood-frame Prairie house for them in Highland Park, Illinois.[2] Years later, after her husband died, she moved to Southern California, where in 1923 Wright designed for her a three-story, all-concrete residence that he nicknamed "La Miniatura," Spanish for "The Miniature."

Although this house, at 2,400 square feet, is not one of his larger residences in Southern California, it certainly does not give one the impression of being small. Wright's use of the secluded, lushly landscaped one-acre site, on the cusp of a small ravine, was masterful. Situated at the end of a cul-de-sac in a quiet, upscale neighborhood, the house is set well back from the street, down a wide, tree-shaded concrete path. The solid massing of the house, its setback lines, geometric patterns along the walls, and the blending of the building into the almost jungle-like setting combine to create the effect of a well-preserved ancient Mayan temple when first seen from the curb. The feeling this romantic composition evokes is simply magical.

The first feature that greets visitors to the Millard House is a tall two-car garage at the end of the driveway, with antique, carved-oak doors that display a Moorish-looking decorative pattern.

FACING: Millard House, Pasadena, California (1923–24), view toward entryway from garden.

Above: Millard House, view of garage. Facing: Millard House, view from guesthouse to main house.

The bedroom has high ceilings and tall, narrow windows on the east wall, which look out onto the lushly planted front yard. The bathroom has concrete block walls with incised cross patterns, as do most of the interior walls throughout the house. The floors in the main house, and in the guesthouse/studio in the back, are made of concrete slabs scored in a four-foot-square pattern, a technique Wright would use on his later Usonian houses throughout the United States.

Between the living room and the entry-level bedroom is a set of stairs that leads down to the formal dining room on the bottom level. The walls in this room are made of plain concrete, and there is a small fireplace set into the east wall. On the west wall, Wright placed French doors leading out onto a concrete patio that adjoins the garden. A concrete footpath running along the northern edge of the garden connects the main house to a two-story guesthouse/studio at the rear of the lot. Behind the dining room is the kitchen, with an adjoining pantry in the southeast corner. There is also a small full bath in the northeast corner of this level, with a maid's room to the left. Wright included a subterranean entrance to the garage from this lower level.

On the third story of the Millard House, Wright placed the master bedroom suite. This bedroom has a peaceful, pleasing ambience, with its floor-to-ceiling wood-latticed windows overlooking the wooded front yard, and 14-foot-tall ceilings. The large windows that open outward, sylvan views, and ample natural light in this room create the indoor-outdoor effect that Wright was so famous for. The master bath has Delft tiles set into the walls, and an eighteenth-century Italian carved wood door. Millard asked Wright to incorporate some of her antique furnishings into the design of her house, as he did here and on the garage doors. On the fourth, or top, level of the Millard House there is a large, wide concrete deck with a low wall around it, and a sleeping loft along the east side. This deck has marvelous views of the entire property in every direction.

To the left of the garage is a wide concrete patio that leads to the front entrance, which is around the side of the house, facing north. The double front doors have redwood-framed glass panels. Upon entering the house, an impressive two-story living room greets visitors on the right. This spacious room has a 15-foot-high ceiling, lined with redwood beams and rich paneling. Along the west wall of this room, Wright placed a row of wood-frame glass-paned doors that open out onto a concrete balcony, overlooking the private garden behind the house. The garden is heavily wooded along its edges, and there is a romantic-looking man-made pond in the middle. The walls of the living room are made out of undisguised concrete blocks, set into plain square panels on the south wall. Above the doors Wright placed clear glass transoms, and above these are four rows of concrete blocks with cutout geometric designs in a cross pattern. On the eastern wall of the living room is a tall walk-in fireplace, with a wrought iron grillwork screen and concrete block facing. A long balcony runs along the top of this wall, providing an impressive view of the magnificent living room below. Behind the living room is a bedroom and full bath.

ABOVE, LEFT: Millard House, view from living room balcony. ABOVE, RIGHT: Millard House, detail on second-floor staircase. FACING: Millard House, living room.

Frank Lloyd Wright had also conceived of a two-story guesthouse/studio behind the main residence in his original plans for the Millard House, but the actual design and execution of this building was carried out by his eldest son, Lloyd Wright, in 1926. He incorporated all of his father's design motifs from the main house for this freestanding structure overlooking the garden and pool. The guesthouse/studio is built of textile blocks, with the same geometric motifs pierced or incised into the wall around the front door. The front entrance is on the south side, with tall, glass-paned French doors that open outward. The major room on the first floor is a spacious living room/library, with 15-foot-high, two-story ceilings like the living room in the main house. There is an open dining area adjoining the living room, and a kitchen to the right of it. Off the east end of the living room is a cozy sitting room, with a fireplace faced in concrete blocks. On the upper level, up a narrow set of stairs, are a bedroom and full bath. There is another entrance to the studio on this level: a small door on the east side that is reached down a concrete path that runs between the garage and the main house. This door opens onto a balcony that overlooks the living room. In 2001, Frank Lloyd Wright's grandson Eric Wright supervised a thorough restoration of both

the main house and the guesthouse/studio. The entire property was put on the National Register of Historic Places in 1976.[3]

Many visitors to the Millard House assume that the cross motifs that are incised or pierced into the textile blocks on both buildings are Wright's version of the traditional Christian cross. Actually, Wright adapted this design from Navajo rug patterns. In fact, the entire concept of this project was inspired by the various pre-Columbian Native American cultures that Wright admired and used as the inspiration for many of his residential design features from the 1910s on.

Along the north side of the property there is a wide upper terrace. This serene area can be approached either from a set of concrete steps leading up to it along the north side of the garage, or from a stepping-stone pathway that winds its way from the lower garden between the main house and the studio. At the top of the steps, a pair of crouching stone lions facing west sit atop concrete pedestals, watching people as they leave the terrace. A spacious lawn takes up most of the space in this terrace, with small flower beds and a boxwood border along its south edge. The west and north sides are sheltered by tall bushes and trees, and there is a concrete patio for alfresco dining near the back of the terrace. Stepping stones lead

from the south side of the lawn to a small terrace along the north side of the studio, where a row of windows in the wall overlooks the living room below. The landscaping in the upper terrace was designed by Lloyd Wright in 1926, and he also redesigned much of the landscaping in the lower garden at that time.[4]

The original budget Wright gave Alice Millard for construction of La Miniatura was $10,000. But like most of his other residential commissions, the final cost came to much more; in this case, $70,000. Soon after Millard moved into her house, the basement flooded during heavy rains due to inadequate storm drains, so she had to have the drains enlarged. The first reaction of local critics and other area architects to the Millard House was negative, and some rivals even expressed outright ridicule. One Beaux-Arts–trained designer said Wright's use of such a common

building material as concrete for the walls of expensive homes caused his associates to break into "howls of laughter." And the *New York Times* asked several years later, "What kind of rich person, many wondered, would want to live in such a house?" But Wright's response was unapologetic: "I would rather have built this little house than St. Peter's in Rome," he insisted. Years later, looking back on his work in the Los Angeles area, he said of his design for the Millard House that it "belonged to the ground on which it stood."[5]

In constructing the concrete blocks used here and in his other Los Angeles–area textile block houses, Frank Lloyd Wright utilized local sand, often from the building site. He believed that this method would ensure that the color and texture of the blocks would blend in with the natural setting of each house. In practice,

By far the largest home Wright designed using the textile block method was the Charles Ennis House, designed in 1923 and located at 2607 Glendower Avenue in the Los Feliz District of Los Angeles. This massive, rambling concrete residence dominates the crest of a steep hillside that overlooks the streets of Hollywood and the Los Angeles Basin far below. The Ennis House rises above the crest of this hill, with long rows of setbacks that culminate in a wide central tower. Seen from below, the house has the appearance of a low-lying Mayan pyramid perched atop a hill. This home is a prime example of Wright's fascination with pre-Columbian architecture during the 1920s in Southern California, a style often called "Mayan Revival." Yet as anyone who has visited pre-Columbian

Ennis House, Los Angeles (1923–24), detail of gate.

FACING: Millard House, master bedroom. ABOVE: Millard House, guesthouse interior toward garden.

however, this system created a number of problems. The color and texture of the blocks did not always end up matching that of the sand at the site, and impurities in the local sand led to deterioration of some of the concrete blocks over time. Yet these problems could be seen as analogous to the problems of water leakage in Wright's flat roofs, and the same solution that owners of Wright's houses have adopted for that problem applies with his textile block houses. Regular, diligent maintenance, and the replacement of failing materials as needed, are really the only effective measures to keep ahead of these problems, just as is required for most older homes.

architectural sites in Central America knows, the pyramids were never perched atop steep hills. Thus the Ennis House, like all of Wright's other textile block houses, makes unique use of its natural setting.

The overall impression it creates is that of a romantic retreat high above the mundane world below, where a director of 1920s Hollywood silent films could have lived and shot some of the scenes for his movies. Indeed, this house has been used as the

ABOVE: Ennis House, south façade. RIGHT: Ennis House, living room. Photograph © 1988 Scot Zimmerman.

setting for several Hollywood feature films over the past half century (though no silent films were made here). The exterior of the Ennis House was the setting for the 1959 horror film *House on Haunted Hill*, starring Vincent Price (all the interior scenes were shot on a set that did not resemble Wright's design). In 1975, the house's exterior (and some of the interior) was used again for a scene in the movie *The Day of the Locust.* In the 1982 movie *Blade Runner,* starring Harrison Ford, the Ennis House was used as the place where the main character lived in a futuristic Los Angeles. Some parts of the interior of the house were also used in nearly a dozen other Hollywood films, including *Black Rain, The Glimmer Man, The Replacement Killers, Rush Hour,* and *The Karate Kid, Part III.* The house was also featured in the TV series *Buffy the Vampire Slayer* and *Twin Peaks,* and was the setting for a number of music videos featuring various artists, including Michael Jackson and Ricky Martin.[6]

The front entrance to the Ennis House is on the north side, on Glendower Avenue. The north façade of the home presents a long, low horizontal mass, with rows of textile block walls about 10 feet high along the sidewalk. Wright created a hidden private entrance, which is behind an ornate cast iron grill-work gate, down a set of steps, and beneath a long overhang on the west side. This entrance is to the left of a wide, deep plaza that wraps around the west and south sides of the house. This plaza is cordoned off from the street by the cast iron gate, the design of which was chosen by Mrs. Ennis. The plaza is made out of concrete slabs, scored in square panels. The walls of the house feature textile blocks with plain surfaces alternating with others that have an interlocking geometric pattern with an Aztec-like appearance.

The living space of the Ennis House is quite large. There are actually two buildings on the property: the main house, and a small chauffeur's quarters/garage, which sits at the western edge of the large plaza. The main house has a total of 10,000 square feet of living space on upper and lower levels. A spacious

living room with high ceilings is on the main level. It has a tall leaded glass window facing south, which provides a magnificent view of Hollywood and downtown Los Angeles. Wright designed a wisteria vine pattern for this window, one of his last uses of decorative art glass windows on any residence.[7] There is a fireplace on the north wall of the living room, beyond a loggia formed from tall pillars made out of decorated textile blocks. Running along the east wall of the living room is a deep balcony, which allows the owners to look out over their guests as they arrive. It could also be used as a "musicians' perch" for entertaining during large social gatherings. To the east of the house are two bedrooms and a bath, including the master bedroom. A half level up is the dining room, which faces south to catch the light and the best views. Wright also placed the kitchen, pantry, and a guest bedroom on this upper level. The hallways in the main house are long, gallery-like passageways lined with decorated textile block pillars. They have an appearance of temple or cathedral aisles, but because of Wright's liberal use of tall picture glass windows throughout most of the house, these hallways are much brighter than those in a temple or a church. Wright also used teakwood for the doors and window frames in each room, thus creating a pleasing textural and color

contrast to the dominant beige color and rough texture of the exposed textile block walls.

The south façade of the Ennis House is quite impressive. The two-story main house rises above the steep hillside in an imposing, horizontal mass. Below the house itself is a 20-foot-tall retaining wall, also made of textile blocks, to help stabilize the massive structure. The tall, leaded-glass picture window with its wisteria motif set into the south wall of the living room stands out from the street below. These features make this house the most visually arresting structure on the entire hillside. Construction of the main house and the chauffeur's quarters was completed in 1924. A subsequent owner, John Nesbit, had Wright add a swimming pool on the north terrace, and a billiards room on the ground floor.

Despite its huge retaining wall, the house had serious structural problems even before construction was complete. Some of the concrete blocks cracked, and the lower sections of the walls buckled from the stress of the weight above them. This problem was due in large part to impurities in the crushed granite that was mixed to make the concrete, and partly due to air pollution, which was bad in Los Angeles even in the 1920s.[8] A protective coating was applied to the walls in an attempt to solve this problem, which

Facing: Ennis House, north façade. Above: Ennis House, view of plaza with chauffeur's quarters on right.

slowed down the decay of the textile blocks but did not stop it. By the time of the Northridge earthquake of 1994, many of the concrete blocks were failing badly, and the quake exacerbated the problem.[9]

The eighth owner of the Ennis House, August Brown, donated the house to the Los Angeles nonprofit Trust for Preservation of Cultural Heritage in 1980. The trust, which later changed its name to the Ennis House Foundation, set about the task of raising funds for the restoration of the house. The home was unoccupied for several years because of the structural damage. The Ennis House Foundation calculated it would cost $5 million to stabilize the house, and $15 million for a full restoration.

In 2006, a FEMA grant was issued and a private bank loan secured, and the restoration project began. This project included creating a new structural support system, repairing damaged windows, replacing the damaged concrete blocks, and installing a new roof. The work was completed in 2007 at a cost of $6.4 million, but the public was still not allowed access to the house. The Ennis House Foundation put the house on the market in 2009.[10]

In July 2011, the Ennis House was sold to business executive Ron Burkle for a little under $4.5 million. Burkle had experience with restoring and maintaining historic homes in the Los Angeles area, having previously owned Greenacres, the home of silent film comedian Harold Lloyd, for several years. Burkle began the process of completing the necessary repairs that the Ennis House Foundation had been unable to complete. At the time of this writing this work was still in progress. As part of the terms of the sale, Burkle has agreed to allow the public to have access to the house 12 days a year, once all of the restoration work has been completed.

Frank Lloyd Wright's residential architecture is almost always associated with low-lying, ground-hugging shapes. The most readily recognizable feature of most of his houses is their horizontal massing and sweeping horizontal lines. But on a steep upslope lot in the Hollywood Hills, near the mouth of Laurel Canyon and a few blocks above Sunset Boulevard, Wright designed a very vertical house for John Storer in 1923. The main façade of this three-level house faces south, and is dominated by a row of four two-story-tall concrete pillars that draw one's eye upwards from the entry-level concrete terrace to the flat roof. These pillars line a wall made of wood-frame latticed windows, allowing visitors to see directly into the dining room and the living room above. This creates a most dramatic visual effect as one approaches the house from the curb, giving the Storer House by far the most impressive façade in a neighborhood full of upscale homes.

John Storer was a homeopathic physician from Wisconsin who moved to Los Angeles to try to establish a practice in booming Southern California. After failing the California state medical

FACING: Storer House, Los Angeles (1923–24), south façade. RIGHT: Storer House, view of front terrace.

examination, he turned to real estate, at which he was successful. He hired Wright to design a new home for him that would reflect his new financial status. The lot he bought in 1922 was in a new subdivision that was attracting up-and-coming business people. Wright's design for Storer's home was a reworking of a home he had designed earlier for Charles P. Lowes that was never built.[11] The overall effect of this house is that of a Mayan temple partially hidden amongst exotic jungle vegetation. Mature eucalyptus trees tower above the house along the rear of the property, and thick stands of bamboo line the driveway on the east side of the lot. It was Wright's intention to create an impression of the house being a man-made extension of landscape. However, when construction was completed in 1924, this section of the Hollywood Hills did not have the lush vegetation that it has today. Wright gave his son Lloyd the task of designing the landscaping, as well as supervising the construction, but it would be many years before the romantic,

almost tropical ambience of the setting would be realized. The Mayan influence is reflected in the cutout cross motifs recessed into many of the concrete blocks on the interior and exterior walls. This motif is similar to the one Wright used on the Millard House. The house has a total of 2,967 square feet of living space, with five bedrooms and three baths.[12]

The Storer House is approached via a curved driveway that winds up to a one-car garage on the east end of the house. This garage is made out of the same concrete blocks as the main house, with stained redwood doors that have coffered panels. There is a small entrance on this side of the house, but the main entrance is set into the wall of two-story windows along the south façade. The front door is near the west end of a concrete terrace that runs along the south side of the house, which contains a shallow pool with a small fountain in the middle, enhancing the romantic effect. This wall of windows admits lots of natural light in

FACING: Storer
House, view
of north façade
with pool.
ABOVE: Storer
House, dining
room. RIGHT:
Storer House,
stairwell
looking towards
bedrooms.

the morning, thus bathing the rooms on the south side of the home in the abundant sunlight that is so common in Southern California.

The front door leads directly into a formal dining room. Here Wright's use of his favorite technique of compression and release is quite effective. The dining room has a low ceiling, with elegant polished redwood paneling and open beams. The north wall has the same tall, latticed windows as the south side, with a door that opens onto a large, private concrete terrace surrounded by trees and shrubs. There is a long, narrow swimming pool in the middle of this terrace now, where Wright had originally intended to place a sunken garden. Adjacent to the dining room at the east end of the house is a small kitchen, with cabinets designed by Eric Wright during a 1980s restoration. There is also a bedroom and full bath in this wing. At the west end of the dining room is a freestanding fireplace and flue, faced with concrete blocks. Wright

ABOVE: Storer House, living room looking west. FACING: Storer House, living room from balcony.

created a cozy nook in front of this fireplace, with built-in bookshelves lining the stairwell that leads to the upper levels. The floor of the dining room is made of textured concrete in 18-inch-square panels. Some of the wall sconces in this room and the upper levels are original Wright designs.

The main staircase at the west end of the house is made of concrete, and has wide landings that provide views over the dining room, and of the living room above. On the second-level, halfway up the staircase, Wright placed two spacious bedrooms, with a full bath between them. The stairs continue on up to the grand living room, with its 16-foot-tall ceilings. The same polished redwood panels and open beams were used here as below. The wood-latticed windows here, however, have leaded geometric patterns across the top. In the northwest corner is a concrete fireplace with a wide hearth, and a flue that is decorated with quoining patterns at the corners and on the front. The windows along the north wall look out over the terrace behind the house. Wright designed a passageway between the back of the fireplace and these windows, so that one would emerge into the tall space of the living room in the most impressive way. He also designed a raised landing on the west wall that overlooks the entire room. This landing opens onto a large concrete roof deck, similar to the one he placed on the top level of the Millard House. The floors in the living room are oak. One of the most pleasing features of the Storer House is the large private deck Wright placed off the east end of the living room, above the garage. The deck is shaded by rows of blue and yellow fabric panels lining a metal canopy, a restoration of an original Wright design.[13] This colorful canopy creates a cheerful space for alfresco dining, reading, or relaxing.

John Storer did not live in this house for very long; he sold it in 1927. The wife of architect Rudolph Schindler, Pauline, rented the house for a while after that. The house passed through several owners during the next few decades, including Charles and Helen Druffel, for whom Wright designed some alterations to block out the views of the new homes being built around it. In 1984, noted Hollywood producer Joel Silver bought the house and immediately began a full restoration of the house and grounds to make up for the years of deferred maintenance. This

was done under the supervision of Eric Wright and Martin Weil, former president of the Los Angeles Conservancy. During this project, many of the original concrete blocks were replaced with new blocks made with soil from the backyard mixed with concrete, thus remaining faithful to Wright's original concept of the house as an extension of the landscape. When the restoration work was completed, the *New York Times* declared that the Storer House "is widely considered the best-preserved Wright building in Los Angeles."[14]

Joel Silver sold the house in 2002. At the time of this writing, the current owners had decided to put the house on the market, after living there happily for 11 years. The John Storer House was added to the National Register of Historic Places in 1971.

FACING: Storer House, view from living room onto terrace looking east.
BELOW: Freeman House, Los Angeles (1923–25), detail of eucalyptus pattern in concrete.

RIGHT: Samuel and Harriet Freeman, c. 1930. University of Southern California School of Architecture, Freeman House Archive.
FAR RIGHT: Freeman House, c. 1925. University of Southern California School of Architecture, Freeman House Archive.
FACING: Freeman House, c. 1925. University of Southern California School of Architecture, Freeman House Archive.

▼ ▼ ▼ ▼ ▼

If the Storer House is the best-preserved Wright building in Los Angeles, then the Samuel and Harriet Freeman House, located in a nearby section of the Hollywood Hills, is just the opposite. Serious damage to the interior and exterior of the Freeman House has accumulated over the years from a variety of causes: acid rain, settlement, water seepage, two earthquakes, and vandalism. In 1984, Harriet Freeman deeded the house to the University of Southern California School of Architecture. After her death in 1986, USC began a valiant effort to repair the damage that had already occurred to the home and restore it for possible use as a learning center open to the public. But an unfortunate combination of two earthquakes within seven years, university budget cuts, heavy rains, and the Great Recession have taken a visible toll on the house, and reversed the effects of much of the work the university had completed since the late 1980s. At the time of this writing, the Freeman House is badly in need of millions of dollars of restoration, which USC hopes to secure the funding for in the next few years. Yet the house has been saved from demolition, and is used by the university as a teaching tool for its students. As author Jeffrey Chusid states in his book *Saving Wright,* "It continues to be a valuable pedagogical tool for the School of Architecture, a rich source for seminars and theses."[15]

Samuel and Harriet Freeman were a young married couple who were avid supporters of the arts and left-wing politics. Harriet moved to Los Angeles from the East Coast in 1920, joining her family after touring the country with a dance troupe. She hoped to establish a career in entertainment, but that path did not pan out for her. In 1921, Harriet married Samuel Freeman, a successful jewelry salesman who sold real estate on the side. In 1923, she visited her sister's school on Olive Hill, not far from the Barnsdall House, which Wright had recently completed. After seeing Wright's buildings on Olive Hill, Harriet convinced Samuel that they should commission Frank Lloyd Wright to design their new home. "After seeing Wright's buildings there," Harriet told the *Los Angeles Times* in 1984, "I couldn't imagine choosing another architect."[16]

The site the Freemans chose for their house was a narrow, steep, upslope lot at 1962 Glencoe Way, in the lower Hollywood Hills. Theirs would be the first residence on this hillside. Today the

lower level. Rudolph Schindler designed a studio apartment beneath the garage on the lower level in the 1930s.[17]

The narrow lot was a challenge for Wright, who answered it by designing the house to fit vertically into the hillside in a series of terraced setbacks, and yet giving the house an overall horizontal emphasis by his use of bands of horizontal metal mullions along the windows that compose the corners of the house, as well as a flat roof with wide, overhanging eaves, orienting the terraced levels of the home on an east–west axis, and extending patios and balconies off the southern side. The net effect is to give the house Wright's classic horizontal appearance, despite being set into a narrow lot near the top of a steep hillside.

The front entrance to the Freeman House is in the northeast corner beneath a sheltering overhang that connects to the one-car garage. The compression-and-release effect was used here, with a low ceiling in the entry hall that leads past the kitchen and opens into the impressive living room, with its high ceiling and walls of windows lining the corners on the south side. These windows have 45-degree mitered corners, which give this room the impression of being suspended high above downtown Hollywood, with a superb

house is hemmed in between two homes that are close to the lot lines, and it sits at a bend in the road, with the garage wing running north–south and the front façade running east–west. At 1,200 square feet, the Freeman House is the smallest of Wright's concrete block houses, with a living room, kitchen, and garage on the entry level, and two bedrooms, a full bath, and a lounge on the view of busy Highland Avenue far below. Here Wright placed perforated concrete blocks, with stylized eucalyptus patterns set into them, on either side of French doors that lead onto a small, step-down balcony off the living room. The north wall of the living room has a small fireplace, with inglenook benches flanking it. The walls here are all made out of exposed concrete blocks, with the decorative eucalyptus pattern. The ceiling was made of stained plywood, and Wright placed a light well down the center of the room, with the same cutout pattern as on the south wall used on a clerestory at the top of this light well. This was a feature he would use on his Usonian houses decades later, although then he mostly used wood to line those clerestories. The floors in the living room are made of oak. The floors on the downstairs level are made of concrete slabs in 18-inch-square patterns. On this level, Wright placed the same mitered-corner walls of windows with horizontal mullions as on the upstairs level. The ceilings downstairs are lower than those in the living room.

Wright's plans for the Freeman House were drawn in late 1923 and early 1924, and his son Lloyd helped on the final set of working drawings. Construction began in March 1924, and was completed in March 1925. Lloyd Wright was the supervising architect, and he also designed the landscaping of the patios and terraces so as to make them appear to be a part of the hillside.

After the Freemans moved into the house, they hired Rudolph Schindler to design a studio apartment below the garage for guests. Schindler also designed all the built-ins and most of the freestanding furniture in the house during the 1920s and '30s.[18] The original built-in furniture remains in the house. During the next 55 years, the Freemans had many famous guests visit or stay in their home, including bandleader Xavier Cugat, actors Claude Rains and Helen Walker, dancer and choreographer Martha Graham, photographer Edward Weston, architect Richard Neutra, and Augustus Hawkins, the first African American from California to serve in the U.S. Congress.[19]

Samuel Freeman died in 1980, while Harriet continued to live in the house and entertain distinguished guests until her death in 1986 at age 96. They were estranged during the last several years of their marriage, and lived in separate sections of the house. However, they never divorced, and there is some evidence that this was because neither one wanted to give up the privilege of living in the house Wright had designed for them.[20] After Harriet died, the house was occupied for a while by USC architecture professor and author Jeffrey Chusid, who documented the restoration work on the house in the 1980s and 1990s.[21] When the foundation work

Above: Freeman House, front entrance. Facing: Freeman House, downstairs bedroom with mitered windows.

began, Chusid had to move out. The house is currently occupied by a caretaker and his family while it awaits a benefactor with enough appreciation for the historical and cultural value of this irreplaceable piece of American architectural history to help pay for its restoration, for the benefit of future generations.

CHAPTER 4
FROM THE COAST TO THE DESERT
Other Southern California Houses

"We hope to make this home one of fundamental beauty, and of functional patterns to supply our needs, both material and intangible."

— Mildred Ablin, in a letter to Frank Lloyd Wright, 1958

After completing his last textile block house in the 1920s, Wright never used this method again on any of his houses in California. Instead, between 1939 and 1959, he designed four very different homes in Southern California that are as varied as the unique landscapes they occupy. These houses range from a magnificent retreat perched atop the mountains above Malibu to a spacious and light-filled family home on the edge of the Mojave Desert.

The Santa Monica Mountains rise steeply from the Pacific Coast Highway above Malibu, reaching elevations of over 2,200 feet at their highest peaks. Their rugged, craggy slopes have, as of yet, remained unspoiled, with only a handful of modern McMansions sprinkled amidst the few older ranches and historic homes that were built before the 1950s. Amongst these older homes is the Arch Oboler Gatehouse and Retreat, a group of buildings designed by Frank Lloyd Wright in 1940 and 1941, with various additions and alterations made between 1944 and 1955. The setting of this compound is one of the most spectacular of any of Wright's residences. The site is a 107-acre tract in an unincorporated section of Los Angeles County, at 32436 West Mulholland Highway. The land is spread out across a range of rocky peaks and crags, with valleys and level areas in between. The elevation of the site varies from about 2,000 feet to over 2,200 feet above sea level. The view from

every part of this tract is magnificent, particularly at sunset, with the slopes of the mountains cascading down towards the Pacific Ocean in the distance, where the bright California sun often fills the sky with reds, pinks, and purples on a clear day.

Arch Oboler was a Hollywood producer, director, and screenwriter, who also wrote scripts for radio, including the popular 1930s program *Lights Out.* He knew Frank Lloyd Wright, having been hired to provide film projectors for Wright's private movie theater at Taliesin West. About 1940, he decided he wanted to build a retreat and residence in the Santa Monica Mountains, one that would include post-production facilities and a writing studio. Lloyd Wright found the perfect site, and after Oboler purchased

FACING: Arch Oboler Compound, Malibu, California (1940–55), guesthouse (Eleanor's Retreat). RIGHT: Oboler Compound, elevations of gatehouse. Copyright © The Frank Lloyd Wright Foundation, Scottsdale, Arizona.

Oboler Compound, looking north with gatehouse in distance.

it, he commissioned the elder Wright to design a gatehouse, residence, retreat/guesthouse, stables, office, and children's playrooms. Over the next four years, most of these facilities took shape, but the main house was never built. The gatehouse was completed in 1940, the retreat in 1941, and the additions to the gatehouse were built between 1944 and about 1955. Oboler's mercurial financial fortunes, which rose and fell with his various film ventures, kept him from being able to afford the cost of the primary residence Wright had designed for him. The fittingly romantic name Oboler gave to this compound was Eagle Feather, and he named the studio after his wife, calling it Eleanor's Retreat.[1]

The approach to the Oboler Compound is down a long, level driveway lined with walls made from fieldstone (or as Wright called it, rubblestone) in a variety of colors and textures taken from the site. This was the same material Wright used on most of the exterior walls throughout the rest of the compound. At the end of this driveway is a wide parking pad on the left, and the gatehouse is on the right. The gatehouse is actually one wing of a modified T-shaped group of structures that are under one roof.

The gatehouse itself runs east–west, and its long northern wall has a row of stone pillars that protrude about two feet above the roofline, which creates the impression of an ancient Middle Eastern fortress or the battlements of a Medieval castle on a mountaintop.

The various structures at Eagle Feather display organic design features and a use of natural materials similar to those Wright had used for his own compound at Taliesin West in the Arizona desert. During the late 1930s and early 1940s, Wright developed a highly personal genre called "desert aesthetic," for architecture in arid climates, such as Arizona and Southern California. For masonry walls, he used local stone set into concrete that made them appear to have grown right out of the desert terrain. He also used wood siding on upper walls and low-angled or flat rooflines with wide overhanging eaves that made the buildings seem to nestle comfortably into the landscape. This system was used on the Rose Pauson House in Phoenix, Arizona, designed in 1939, as well as later homes in other parts of the West, such as the Berger House in San Anselmo, California, designed in 1950 (see Chapter 6). The Oboler Compound displays all these characteristics, especially when viewed from above, where it seems to be an extension of the natural landscape. Wright's use of rubblestone pillars, interspersed with sections of picture glass windows and doors, creates a strong rhythmic quality, as does the inward tapering of the upper walls, and sheathing them in cedar clapboards (redwood was used originally, but replaced after it cracked in the dry climate).

The gatehouse wing contains the main living quarters, with a small living room and adjacent open kitchen to the left. This space has a warm, intimate feel, with a fireplace faced with rubblestone on the east wall, a cedar plank ceiling that tiers upward in the middle, and recessed lighting in the kitchen lined with cutout geometric patterns in wood. To the left of the kitchen is a bedroom and full bath. From the

ABOVE: Oboler Compound, south façade. BELOW: Oboler Compound, looking west.

living room there is a superb view of the Pacific Ocean on clear days. The current owners describe this comfortable living space as "a small work of art—a gem."[2]

The children's wing originally had an open staircase (later enclosed) that led to a children's theater and a playroom downstairs. This wing has two levels, with the first level partially set into the gentle upslope hillside on which it sits. A rubblestone fireplace is set into the west wall on both levels, and steel-framed glass doors on the south end open out onto a terrace on the ground level. Upstairs, steel-framed banded picture windows across the upper wall provide a lovely view of a man-made pond below, which was part of the original landscape design done by Lloyd Wright. The ceilings in this wing are similar to those in the gatehouse, with coffered cedar planks, and the same geometric cutout patterns on recessed lighting set into them. There are two bedrooms and two baths on the upper level of this wing, and the theater and

playroom are now being used as a family entertainment and media room. The original stable wing, running east–west off the carport, has been converted into a workroom with a kitchen and office, and also includes a laundry room, bedroom, bath, and sitting area.

The most impressive structure in the Oboler Compound is Eleanor's Retreat. This is a small, separate structure that crowns the top of a craggy outcrop of rock near the southeast corner of the property. Wright designed it to be a self-contained unit for use as a guesthouse, or as a workspace or retreat for Eleanor. The main space is a light-filled open room with panoramic views of the Santa Monica Mountains from picture windows on the east, south, and west sides. A large open-hearth fireplace made of rubblestone and concrete dominates the north side of this room, with a full bath behind it. The floors are made of rubblestone, and two narrow windows on the west wall flank the fireplace, with a built-in desk below one of them and built-in shelving in the corners and along the walls. The

Oboler Compound, children's wing looking south.

Oboler Compound, view through breezeway looking west.

roof is flat, with wide, overhanging eaves that jut far out over the west end. The outer walls are sheathed in cedar planks, with rubblestone for the lower walls. Stone was also used to construct the staircase and the retaining wall leading up to the doorway on the north side and the terrace running along the north and east sides.

Wright's apprentice John Lautner oversaw the construction of the Oboler Compound. Wright came to the site in 1941, after Eleanor's Retreat was completed. He was unhappy with the way Lautner had situated the staircase, so he had some of his "boys" from Taliesin West rebuild the stairs and retaining wall to run north–south in a straight line along the hillside.[3]

Arch and Eleanor Oboler lived in the compound for several years, during which Arch worked on several small-budget Hollywood films. These included a 1951 science fiction movie, *Five,* which was shot at and around the compound, about a group of post–nuclear war survivors. He also worked on the film *Bwana Devil,* the first-ever feature-length 3-D movie in color. Arch died in 1987, and Eleanor remained on the property for a few more years.[4] The compound was put on the market after her death, and it nearly met a sad fate when a developer bid on it, with plans to divide the property into 15 lots for luxury homes. His offer was accepted, but was withdrawn due to the housing crisis of the early 1990s.[5]

In 1996, Dorothy and John Knight bought the Oboler Compound. Since then, they have been engaged in a major restoration of the property, including

ABOVE: Oboler Compound, guesthouse looking south. BELOW: Oboler Compound, blueprint of guesthouse floor plan. Copyright © The Frank Lloyd Wright Foundation, Scottsdale, Arizona.

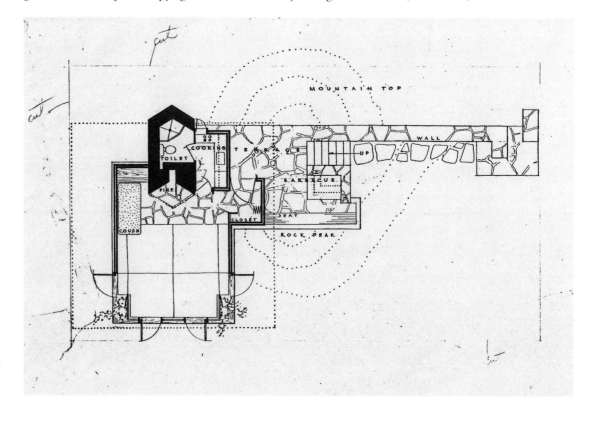

ABOVE: Oboler Compound, guesthouse bedroom looking east. BELOW: Oboler Compound, detail of guesthouse fireplace. FACING: Sturges House, Brentwood, California (1939), view from north.

repairing the damage from years of deferred maintenance. They have also done lots of landscaping work on the site, such as removing a pool that Arch Oboler had installed near the gatehouse, and putting in the large pond below Eleanor's Retreat. They plan to bring this marvelous piece of California's architectural heritage back to its full aesthetic beauty.

▼ ▼ ▼ ▼ ▼

At the top of a wide, upslope lot in the tony Los Angeles suburb of Brentwood, two miles west of Beverly Hills, sits a home that is dramatically different from all of its neighbors. The George D. Sturges House, designed and built in 1939, is one of Frank Lloyd Wright's most futuristic-looking West Coast residences. This one-story house appears to be hovering over its hillside lot: the entire east end of the house is cantilevered out over the site, thus presenting the most prominent profile of any home in this neighborhood. At the time it was built, this was a radical design for a house, even for avant-garde Southern California. Beginning in the late 1950s, streamlined homes jutting out over upslope sites began to be a common feature in hillside communities all over California. But in 1939, there were very few such houses anywhere on the West Coast.

The use of sweeping cantilevered masses projecting out over the

Above: Sturges House, view of north façade with carport. Facing: Sturges House, west façade view of entrance.

landscape had first been employed by Wright on Fallingwater, the home he had designed in 1936 for Edgar Kaufmann in Pennsylvania. Though the sites are very different, the Sturges House, at 449 N. Skyewiay Road, has the same extended horizontal lines and dramatic profile that Fallingwater does. This type of design was Wright's response to America's fascination with speed and motion in the 1930s. Indeed, the Sturges House, with its wide projecting deck springing forward from a brick and concrete base, almost appears to be in motion. Wright's use of kiln-dried redwood clapboarding along the exterior walls adds to the horizontal emphasis, and accentuates this effect. The square base and the rectangular massing of the brick-faced upper façade create a Cubist-like rhythm that counterbalances the cantilevered deck. Wright hired John Lautner to be the supervising architect for the construction of this innovative residence.

The Sturges House is one of Wright's smallest homes in California, with only 900 square feet of interior living space. The interior space is supplemented quite effectively by Wright's use of the balcony along the entire east side so that all the living areas are adjacent to it. The deck is 58 1/2 feet long, and 6 1/2 feet deep, thus providing another 380 square feet of usable space during all the warm days and nights that are so common in Southern California.[6] The deck wraps around the southeast corner of the house, providing a side terrace. The living room and two bedrooms have floor-to-ceiling windows that line the deck, and a plate glass door in the living room opens out onto the deck. A wide redwood trellis over the deck provides some shade on hot days, while square openings admit the morning sunlight into the interior. A bathroom, workspace, and utility area are located behind the bedrooms on the north side of the house off a long, gallery-style hallway. A narrow set of exterior stairs on the north side of the house leads from the side terrace to a spacious roof deck, with panoramic views in three directions, including a view of the Pacific Ocean about three miles to the west.

The roof of the Sturges House is flat, and Wright also used overhanging trellises on the west side of the house, where the recessed front door is set into the far south corner. This is a Dutch-style double door, and Wright placed it beneath a solid redwood overhang to shelter it from the elements. A long driveway leads up to this entrance, with a four-car carport running west from it—an unusually large parking space for the 1930s. The front door opens directly into the living room. This is an open rectangular room, with redwood paneling on the north and south walls, built-in wooden seating along the south wall, and a small fireplace on the west wall. The original Wright-designed redwood chairs are still here, and the floors are made out of linoleum in eight-inch-square sections in Wright's favorite Cherokee red color.

The current owner of the Sturges House, former actor Jack Larson, bought the home in 1967. At that time, the house needed major work, including stripping paint off the exterior redwood, removing black paint from the interior walls, and replacing the

leaking tar-and-gravel roof with a new water-resistant high-tech one.[7] At this writing, the house retains all of its original architectural features, and is a rare example of an intact Early Modern California house from the 1930s. It was designated a Historic-Cultural Monument by the City of Los Angeles in 1993.

In the 1998 Hollywood film *Permanent Midnight,* starring Ben Stiller and Elizabeth Hurley, Hurley's character lives in an elegant modern house in the suburban hills above the Los Angeles Basin, with stunning views of the city lights far below. It was the Wilbur C. Pearce House, in the tiny, affluent hillside town of Bradbury. Like a number of other Frank Lloyd Wright houses that were used in feature films, only the exterior scenes were filmed at the actual site, while a set was built for the interior scenes. This was done mostly because the interior of the Pearce House at that time was not well kept, with green paint covering all the original beige-colored concrete block walls, and deteriorating woodwork on the ceilings. A tenant occupied the home for several years, making changes to the décor and allowing deferred maintenance to take its toll. At this writing, however, the Pearce House has been owned for several years by Konrad Pearce, the grandson of the original owner, who has been working meticulously to restore the residence to its historical appearance. It now looks almost the way it did when it was finished in 1955.[8] The house is at 5 Bradbury Hills Road.

Wilbur C. Pearce was a marketing executive with the Firestone Tire and Rubber Company, and his wife, Elizabeth, was an abstract artist and president of the Women's Art League in Akron while they lived in Ohio. The Pearces met Frank Lloyd Wright when Elizabeth invited him to give a lecture to Akron city officials about a proposed art museum. They became friends, and Wright later agreed to design a home for them once they had relocated to California.[9] In 1950, they bought a two-acre lot in the eastern foothills of unincorporated Los Angeles County, with views of the Los Angeles Basin and its city lights to the south, and the undeveloped San Gabriel Mountains and Angeles National Forest to the north. Wright drew up a full set of plans in 1950 for a single-story, two-plus-bedroom, two-bath,

ABOVE: Pearce House, Bradbury, California (1950–55), view of east façade. BELOW: Pearce House, black bear cub swimming in pool on east terrace. Photograph by Konrad Pearce. FACING: Pearce House, east façade looking south.

1,900-square-foot house. Construction did not begin until 1954, and the Pearces moved into the home in 1955. William Wesley ("Wes") Peters, one of Wright's most trusted Taliesin associates, was the supervising architect. Wright's original bid called for a budget of $15,000, but

like so many of his other residential designs, the final cost was much more—in fact, it came to double that original figure.[10]

The Pearce House is a variation of Wright's Usonian-style homes. In essence, this was Wright's attempt to create a system of supposedly affordable, detached housing for middle-class families. These homes were all designed on a variant of a grid pattern, usually using square modules for the floor plans, and incorporating a number of signature features such as carports and concrete slab floors. The Pearce House is a bit different than most Usonian houses; here, Wright used a pattern of segmented circles for the floor plan and the exterior of the home. He had used this design module on a handful of earlier homes, such as the second Herbert and Katherine Jacobs House in 1944 in Middleton, Wisconsin, and the Kenneth and Phyllis Laurent House in 1949 in Rockford, Illinois.

The materials Wright used on the Pearce House were concrete block for the walls, plate glass for the doors and windows, Douglas

ABOVE: Pearce House, view of gallery looking south. BELOW: Pearce House, view of living room/dining room looking north. RIGHT: Pearce House, view of living room with fireplace with green paint on concrete blocks. Photograph © 1988 Scot Zimmerman.

ABOVE: Pearce House, master bedroom looking south. FACING: Pearce House, north façade with carport.

fir for the ceilings, and Honduran mahogany overlay on the window framing. The floors are made of concrete slabs, in three-foot-square patterns, stained Cherokee red. By far the most distinctive feature of the house is Wright's use of a sweeping concave curve along the fascia on the south side. The fascia on the north side has a slight convex curve to it. All the fascias are several inches wide, creating a strong visual line at the end of the wide overhanging eaves that extend around the entire perimeter of this flat-roofed home. These eaves partially shade two terraces. The north terrace, off the living room, is in the shape of a pointed arch. The south terrace runs nearly the entire length of the house, following the curve of the fascia. There is a small pool set into the middle of this terrace, which Wright called the promenade. Konrad Pearce told me he has seen a family of black bears, a mother and her three cubs who often come down from the Angeles National Forest at dusk, playing in this pool (undoubtedly not the use Wright originally intended for it). At the east end of the house is a two-car carport beneath extended overhangs, and an adjacent workshop and half bath. (The workshop was designed to be used as Elizabeth's painting studio, but it was too dark, so she used one of the bedrooms instead.) Konrad recalls that his grandparents told him the original tar-and-gravel roof did not leak for the first 10 years they lived there.[11]

The main entrance to the house is on the northeast end. The plate glass front door opens directly into the living room, which is a wide, open space that doubles as the dining room. Wright placed a wall of floor-to-ceiling windows on both the south and north sides of this room. A glass door opens from the southeast corner of the room out onto the curved terrace. Another glass door opens out onto the north terrace. Elizabeth asked Wright to alter his original plans for the windows on the north side to allow for a full view of the mountains. So Wright raised the height of the ceiling on this side so that the overhanging eaves would not cut off the view.[12] The ceiling in most of the living room is seven feet ten inches tall, with wood paneling between open beams. At the north end, the ceiling is two feet higher, with a plain glass clerestory running east–west around the edge of this raised section. A fireplace faced with concrete block is set into the east wall, and there are built-in bookshelves lining the northeast corner of the room. There is also a low built-in seat that runs along the wall between the fireplace and the northeast corner.

At the west end of the living room is a wood-sided service core that rises from the floor to the ceiling, with cabinets set into it and built-in shelves lining the north side. Behind this is a small kitchen,

or as Wright called it, a workspace, with mahogany overlay cabinets and countertops. To the left of the service core is a long gallery that runs most of the length of the south side of the house. There is built-in shelving along the inner wall of the gallery, and the outer wall of floor-to-ceiling windows creates a pleasing indoor-outdoor effect, bathing the interior with natural light. The gallery connects the two bedrooms: a small bedroom in the middle of the house, and the master bedroom suite at the far west end. The master bedroom has floor-to-ceiling picture windows on the south wall, and narrow-slit wood-frame windows on the north wall. There is a small, adjacent full bath, and there are built-in storage cabinets along the north wall, as there also are on the north wall of the smaller bedroom.

The engineering of the Pearce House was supervised by Wes Peters, while the overall supervising architect was another of Wright's most trusted associates from Taliesin, Aaron Green. Green reoriented Wright's original placement of the house to avoid the steepest part of its hillside lot, and allow for more space for the workshop/studio wing off the east end.[13] Wilbur and Elizabeth occupied the house until they died, after which their son Llewellyn moved into it in 1985. Then Konrad Pearce obtained title to the property in 2002, and he has been spending much of his spare time since then restoring his grandfather's elegant house to its original condition.

At the edge of the Mojave Desert, near the eastern fringes of the boomtown of Bakersfield, sits the last house Frank Lloyd Wright designed on the West Coast, two months before he died in April 1959. The George Ablin House, at 4260 Country Club Drive, is one of the most spacious and gracious of Wright's several 1950s homes in California. The house sits on a one-and-a half-acre lot, within the grounds of the Bakersfield Country Club. This single-story residence has 3,600 square feet of living space, with five bedrooms, four baths, a living room with a dining area, a kitchen, a study, and a swimming pool in the backyard. The larger-than-usual living space in the Ablin House was the result of a very active correspondence between Wright's Taliesin staff and Dr. Ablin's wife, Mildred, over the last year of Wright's life. George Ablin was one of the most successful neurosurgeons in Bakersfield, which had a population of about 50,000 in the late 1950s.[14]

"Millie" Ablin first wrote to Wright in the summer of 1958,

asking him to design a new home for George and herself and their large family. In a letter dated June 10, 1958, she stated:

We were wondering if it is possible for you and practical for us to have you design a home for us and our young family of six, and probably seven children (see enclosed picture—youngest is 8 and $^1/_2$ years). We have a steep hillside lot (100 x 340) with an excellent view overlooking the community itself and the surrounding country, at the edge of the Mojave Desert, with mountains always prominently visible. We hope to make this home one of fundamental beauty, and of functional patterns to supply our needs, both material and intangible.[15]

ABOVE: Millie Ablin and Frank Lloyd Wright at Taliesin West, February 1959. Courtesy of Ablin Family Collection. BELOW: Ablin House, Bakersfield, California (1958–61), west façade. FACING: Ablin House, wall of windows outside living room.

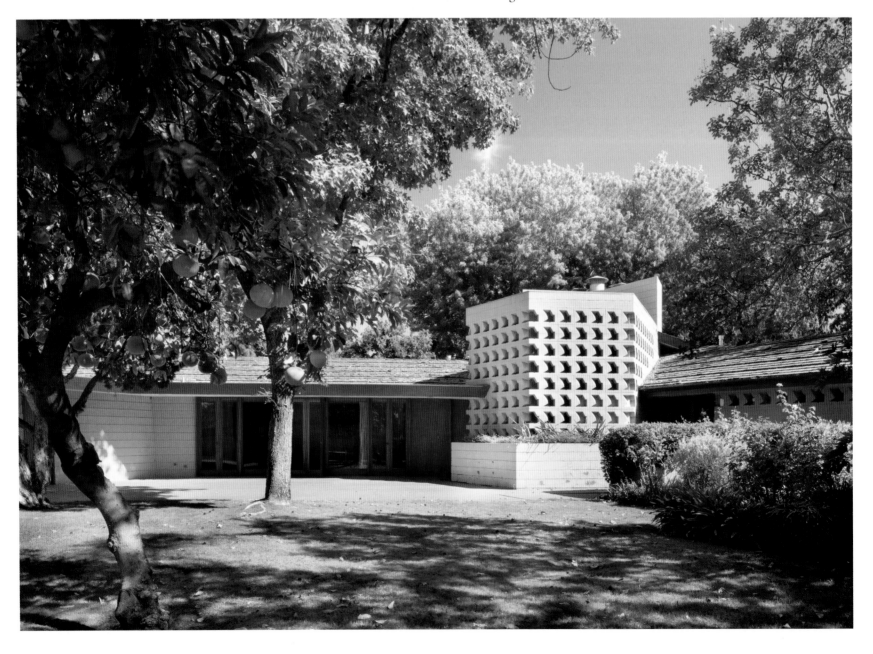

Ablin House, east façade.

Facing: Ablin House, dining area with Frank Lloyd Wright–designed table and chairs. Above: Ablin House, full view of living room.

Wright's chief draftsman, John Howe, wrote back promptly, asking for more information about the property and the Ablins' requirements. So Millie sent him a topographical map and some 35 mm slides of the property. Wright's executive secretary, Eugene Masselink, then responded with a letter telling them that "Mr. Wright" would draw up a preliminary set of plans for their house. After receiving these plans, Millie wrote another letter to Wright on January 7, 1959, asking him to make a total of 15 changes to his original design. Wright was famous for being resistant to making many changes in his plans (see the sections on the Buehler House in Chapter 5 and the Walker House in Chapter 6), so the Ablins had no way of knowing if he would accept their request. Among the changes they asked for were twin built-in beds in the master bedroom; double sinks in the master bathroom; carpeting in the adult living wing, living room, and dining area; extra storage cabinets throughout the house; and a fence around the pool in the backyard for the safety of their children. Of these items, Wright did agree to design the twin beds, the double sinks, and the extra storage throughout the home.[16]

In February 1959, Millie and George Ablin visited Frank Lloyd Wright at his studio at Taliesin West. During their visit he suggested they buy a second adjacent lot, so the house could be sited more appropriately, with the living room facing the golf course, and thus providing unspoiled views of the greenery around them. They followed his advice, and he agreed to design an extra bedroom in the children's wing for their seventh child. Wright died on April 10, so the full set of working drawings were actually signed by Wes Peters in May 1959, even though the design of the house was clearly done by Wright himself.[17] The home was completed in 1961. The materials used in its construction were salmon-tinted concrete blocks on the walls, plate glass windows and doors, Philippine mahogany for framing and built-in furniture, wood shingles on the roof, and concrete slabs on the floors in four-by-four-foot patterns stained Cherokee red.

The front of the Ablin House faces southeast, and it sits atop a gentle, grassy knoll, with the main entrance in the rear. The triangular-shaped swimming pool is surrounded by a concrete slab deck (but no fence). There is a grassy play area between the pool and the house, and a concrete slab terrace lining the rear walls. The low-gabled rooflines have wide overhanging eaves, which shelter the interior from the harsh Central Valley sun. The floor plan is in the shape of a modified "V," with the entry hall and the kitchen at the apex. To the right, along a gallery-style hall, is a small study and the spacious master suite. To the left, adjoining another gallery, are the children's bedrooms. The narrow entry hall, with its seven-foot-two-inch ceiling, opens into the huge living room, with a soaring ceiling that rises to a fourteen-foot-high peak at the southeast end. The roofline here forms a sharp projecting peak, a feature that Wright used on many of his post–World War II houses on the West Coast.

The most impressive feature of the living room is the 48-foot-wide wall of windows that undulates across the east end. These floor-to-ceiling windows allow this room to be flooded with natural light, and their wood framing, together with the built-in furniture, salmon-colored walls, and red floors, create a very warm and elegant ambience (though the specific tint used on the concrete block walls was a decision made by Taliesin Associated Architects shortly after Wright's death).[18] Two sets of double wood-frame doors are set into this wall of glass, providing access to a spacious terrace surrounded by a low concrete border. In the northeast

Ablin House, west façade with pool.

corner, Wright placed a dining area with a long built-in table and a set of 10 wooden chairs, all of which survive. The use of a far corner of the living room for dining gives this space a feeling of almost being a separate dining room. On the west wall is a wide fireplace. The ceiling is covered in sand-colored acoustic material. In the entry hall leading from the west side into the living room, Wright placed a built-in minibar, a feature requested by the Ablins. Besides the original dining set, the other existing wooden

furniture in the living room, though designed by Wright, was not made until 1992 by Taliesin Associated Architects.[19]

The most distinctive room in the Ablin House is the kitchen. Here, Wright created a space unlike any other he had designed for all of his West Coast houses. This room is contained inside a tall, irregularly shaped concrete cube, whose walls are pierced by dozens of repeated geometric patterns that are glazed on the inside. The effect this creates in the daytime is truly amazing, with the sunlight splashing onto the countertops and across the wide workspace. The appliances here are all original, as are the countertops covered in pink tiles.

The master bedroom and bath are both unusually spacious, compared with most of the other homes Wright designed on the West Coast in the 1950s. There are built-in bookcases and shelves along the walls of the master bedroom, and the bathroom fixtures are all original. The hallway connecting the master suite to the entry area is also quite spacious, with storage cabinets along the walls. Wright also placed storage cabinets all along the walls of the hallway that leads to the children's bedrooms, as well

Ablin House, kitchen.

as designing built-in bookshelves and desks in these bedrooms. A three-car carport runs off the northwest corner of the house, and it connects to a small storage room. The wide overhanging eaves that run around the entire perimeter of the house provide protection from the weather when walking from the carport to the main entrance.

George and Mildred Ablin lived happily in their house for the rest of their lives. They raised seven children there: four sons and three daughters. George died in 1999, and Millie passed away about 2002. A few years later, the house was sold to its current owner, Michael Glick, who has maintained the home in its original condition. The house is occasionally used as a meeting place for various professional groups and conferences, as well as for research by Wright scholars.[20] Thus, the George Ablin House has been preserved as an invaluable cultural resource, and an intact treasure of America's twentieth-century architectural legacy.

CHAPTER 5

A UNIQUE USONIAN
The Buehler House, Orinda, California, 1948-49

"Madame, you do not seem to realize that women have been emancipated from the kitchen."
— Frank Lloyd Wright to Katherine Buehler, 1948

The phone call came quite unexpectedly early one morning. As Maynard and Katherine Buehler later recalled, it was an unusual conversation. When they picked up the phone, a man with a confident tone in his voice said, "This is your architect calling. I'm going to be in San Francisco for a while. I'll be staying at the St. Francis Hotel. Let's meet there for breakfast tomorrow at 8 a.m." It was Frank Lloyd Wright.

Maynard Buehler had written a letter to Mr. Wright, including a photo of the 2.3-acre lot they had purchased in Orinda, asking him to design their home. They got a brief letter from Wright agreeing to their request, then no further communication for several months, so they began looking for another architect. Then, out of the blue, Wright called them. When they asked if the meeting had to be at 8 a.m., Wright responded, "I can make it 7 a.m., if you'd like."[1]

This was the beginning of a very unconventional working relationship between the Buehlers and Frank Lloyd Wright. There would be disagreements over details, occasional construction problems, and more than a little stress. But the end result was a unique Usonian home that Katherine described to me as "a masterpiece." The Maynard P. Buehler House, at just over 4,000 square feet, is the largest Usonian house Wright ever designed on the West Coast. It is also one of the few Wright-designed Usonian homes with a basement. The materials used on the home are not like those in most other Usonian homes: they include dark stained redwood siding

along many of the exterior and interior walls, and gold leaf on the living room, dining room, and master bedroom ceilings.

Prior to contacting Wright, the Buehlers had obtained a bid for designing their house from a prominent San Francisco architect, but they were not satisfied with the design. Katherine had seen an article about the original prototype for Usonian houses, the Jacobs

FACING: Buehler House, Orinda, California (1948–49), living room. RIGHT: Frank Lloyd Wright with workers, c. 1949. Photograph by Joe Monroe.

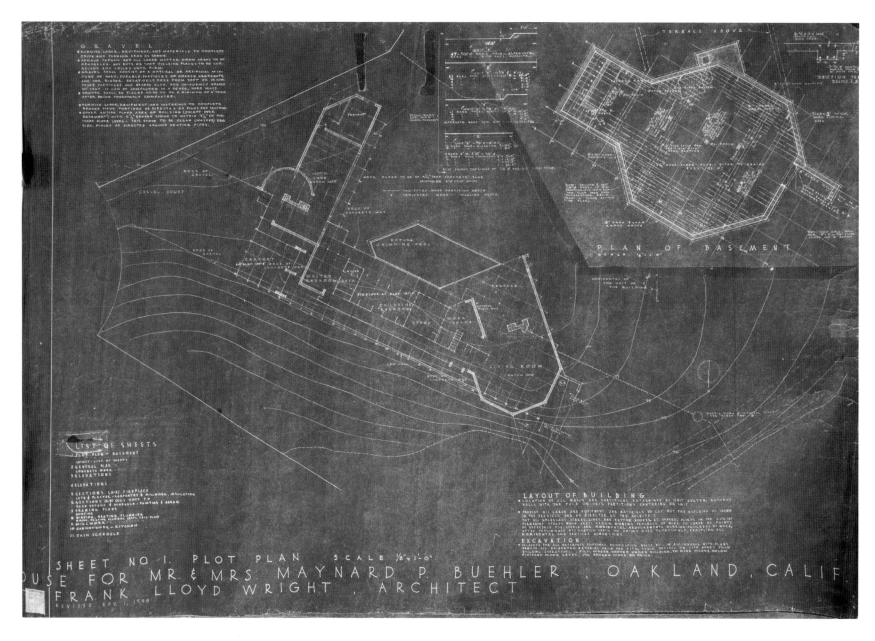

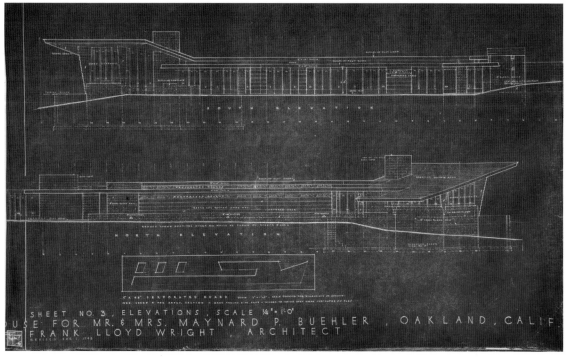

ABOVE: Buehler House, blueprint of plot plan. Copyright © The Frank Lloyd Wright Foundation, Scottsdale, Arizona. LEFT: Buehler House, blueprint of north and south elevations. Copyright © The Frank Lloyd Wright Foundation, Scottsdale, Arizona. FACING: Buehler House, southwest corner.

House in Madison, Wisconsin, in an old magazine. She decided that this innovative and inexpensive type of house design would be ideally suited to the needs of their family and their budget.[2]

The Usonian house was Wright's solution to the needs of a rapidly growing middle class in America. Although its origins date to the mid-1930s, the Usonian style became popular after World War II, and most of Wright's designs in this mode were built between 1945 and 1959. These homes used inexpensive mass-produced materials, such as concrete blocks for walls and concrete slabs for floors, combined with a modular floor plan based on repeated design units, such as hexagons or segments of a circle. These homes often incorporated local materials, and could be easily adapted to the conditions of the building site and the needs of the client. The idea was to provide housing suitable to the needs

of suburban middle-class families while keeping the cost of constructing an architect-designed home down to an affordable level.

Orinda is a peaceful, sylvan bedroom community about 20 miles east of San Francisco, nestled below the eastern slopes of the Berkeley Hills. The lot the Buehlers had purchased was at the end of a quiet cul-de-sac, sheltered by oak and elm trees, with creeks meandering along its east and west edges. The Buehlers wanted their new house located in the southeastern corner of the lot, to take maximum advantage of the wide, tree-shaded lot, which they planned to have beautifully landscaped after the house was finished.

When Wright met the Buehlers at the St. Francis Hotel, he told them he'd already drawn up a preliminary set of plans. After breakfast they went back to his room and he laid out his plans on the bed. Katherine told him that she thought the kitchen was a

ABOVE: Buehler House, west façade. FACING: Buehler House, south façade.

bit too small (small kitchens are common for Usonian houses). Wright replied, "Madame, you do not seem to realize that women have been emancipated from the kitchen." She recalled thinking to herself, "Doggone it! Nobody told me."[3]

That was to be the first of several discussions the Buehlers would have with Wright in which their desires and his ideas for their home did not always mesh. Another such disconnect took place during a driving tour around the North Bay that the Buehlers conducted at Wright's request. The purpose of the tour was to get ideas for materials Wright could use on the exterior of the Buehler House, since Maynard had decided he couldn't afford the Arizona flagstone that Wright had proposed in his original plans. During their drive they passed by a building site near Napa, where a house under construction had a stack of pink concrete blocks piled in the front yard. Wright suggested that they might use that same type of block on their

new house. Maynard later recalled that he said to himself, "Over my dead body you'll put pink blocks on our house!"[4] Being a successful general contractor, Maynard had definite ideas about how he wanted their home to be built, as well as budget limitations that he had to work within. When I interviewed Maynard in June 2001 about his experience of working with Wright on the design of their home, he summed it up this way: "The most accurate word I can use to summarize Wright's overall attitude in talking to us was arrogant."[5]

▼ ▼ ▼ ▼ ▼

After some back-and-forth with the Buehlers about the details and floor plan of their house, Wright drew up a final set of plans dated November 1, 1948. The design is a single-story, L-shaped residence, which embraces a pool on the west side, and has a large living room on the north end with a taller ceiling than usual for Usonian houses. The octagonal living room juts outward at an oblique angle beneath a steeply pitched roofline resembling the prow of a ship. The rest of the house has a nearly flat shed-style roof, including the adjacent dining room in the northwest corner. The walls are made from manufactured concrete block, while the banded windows and doors are framed in redwood. The roof is covered in copper, and the floors are made out of concrete slabs, which are scored with square patterns and stained in one of Wright's favorite colors, Cherokee red. There are two full bathrooms and three bedrooms, including a master bedroom at the south end of the house. A gallery-style hallway along the east side connects the living room with all the bedrooms, a common feature in Usonian homes. The small kitchen is behind the open dining room, with a skylight and a pass-through countertop, so the cook can see the guests in the dining room while at work.

Maynard Buehler reduced Wright's original dimensions along the west end of the house by four feet, to both save money and remove the danger of the Buehlers' two young daughters falling into the pool whenever they stepped into the garden. Wright's plans called for the footprint of the house to be based on four-foot-wide modules, so it was a simple adjustment to reduce the width of the home by four feet along the west side. Wright designed both a full, spacious basement with a high ceiling and a comfortable shop wing for Maynard, who was originally trained as a tool engineer, and had invented a number of gun accessories, such as rifle sights, scopes, and safety locks. So he needed a large workshop with a separate entrance off the south side of the house, not easily accessible to his daughters' bedrooms.[6]

Construction on the Buehler House began in 1949. Wright visited the site only twice: once to inspect the lot and examine the course of the creeks that ran through it, and a second time after the house was completed. One of Wright's most experienced and trusted senior apprentices, Walter Olds, worked with the Buehlers as the supervising architect to carry out the construction of Wright's plans, since Wright was quite busy working on the V. C. Morris Gift Shop in San Francisco at that time, as well as other projects on the West Coast and back East. Olds would later work with the Buehlers again in 1957, when he designed a playhouse for their daughters and a garden house. These structures still stand as they were built, along the west edge of the small garden and the pool, adjacent to the shop wing.[7]

The Buehlers' original budget for the house and shop wing was $25,000. It took about a year to complete construction, and even with the cost-saving features Maynard insisted on, when the project was finally finished, it ended up costing nearly four times their original budget. Shortly after the Buehlers had moved into their new home, Frank Lloyd Wright came by one day, completely unannounced, and rang their doorbell. When they let him in to see his handiwork, without saying a word he simply walked brusquely through each room, pointing toward various features with his cane and nodding. When he was finished with his impromptu inspection, he said to the Buehlers, "Well, it looks like I designed you a beautiful home." Then he turned around and left as abruptly as he had come.[8]

The final phase of the Buehlers' plans called for an intricate landscaping scheme for their two acres of grounds beyond the building site. So they hired renowned Japanese landscape architect Henry Matsutani to design a number of traditional Japanese features for their lot. Matsutani had worked on the grounds of the Imperial Palace in Tokyo before moving to California, where his previous work included refurbishing the Japanese Tea Garden in San Francisco's Golden Gate Park. He worked on the Buehlers' gardens over a period of 37 years, installing such Japanese features as a koi pond where the pool near the house had been, a wooden Japanese footbridge over a stream with a small waterfall, a Japanese-style gazebo, an elegant Japanese teahouse beneath two large overhanging shade trees, and several stone shrines and statues.[9] These landscape features are in complete harmony with Wright's design for the house, since his architectural philosophy was inspired in large part by the features of traditional Japanese residential architecture, which he had first seen when he visited the Japanese Pavilion at the World's Columbian Exposition in Chicago in 1893 while he was working in Louis Sullivan's office.

▼ ▼ ▼ ▼ ▼

During the nearly six decades the Buehlers lived in this house, they made a number of changes to the building, some by choice and

Buehler House, living room with gold ceiling.

some out of necessity. Like all of Wright's other Usonian houses, theirs originally had a gravity heating system, which radiated heat from the floor up through the walls. The purpose of this system was to eliminate radiators and (supposedly) to prevent drafts and temperature changes within the house. But this system never worked efficiently for the Buehlers, perhaps in part because of their unusually large square footage. Another problem, often cited by owners of some of Wright's other houses, was water leakage from the roof—especially around the chimney, but also around the skylight in the kitchen. Some critics have faulted Wright for this very common problem with his residences, especially those

BELOW: Buehler House, gallery-style hallway. RIGHT: Buehler House, dining room.

with flat roofs, which naturally tend to leak more than pitched roofs since they don't shed water as well. But as Andrew L. Owen, a residential and commercial architect in Medford, Oregon, points out, there have been significant improvements in roofing materials and membranes since Wright's time. If these improvements had been available to him, the flat roofs on his houses would probably not have leaked so frequently. There was also a problem in the dining room of the Buehler House, where the glass-paneled coffers in the ceiling radiated too much heat from the sun in warm months, thus making the dining room uncomfortable to sit in during the daytime in spring and summer.[10]

An opportunity to correct these problems, and make other desired changes, came in the form of a tragic accident. One cold day in 1994, the electric heater in Katherine Buehler's bedroom overheated, starting a fire that destroyed the entire bedroom wing and the rear wall of the kitchen. It

also badly charred the living room with its gold-leaf ceiling, as well as destroying the coffered ceiling of the dining room. Katherine still got emotional when she talked to me seven years later about the aftermath of this fire, and seeing her "beautiful home nearly in ruins." But the Buehlers didn't hesitate in deciding to rebuild the house, with some changes they had wanted for a while. They called Walter Olds, now retired and living nearby in Berkeley, to see if he would agree to be their supervising architect again for the restoration of their house. He readily agreed, and the three of them looked over the old blueprints to decide what changes needed

to be made. The Buehlers' daughters were now grown up and on their own, but Maynard and Katherine still liked to entertain guests for dinners and lunches at the dining room set Wright had designed especially for them. It was made from triangular blocks of mahogany, and both the table and chairs Wright designed for it survived the fire. So they set about the task of restoring the house while making modest design changes that were in keeping with Wright's original concept, much as Wright himself had done in remodeling his own residence at Taliesin East. As Olds put it when describing this process in an interview nine years later, "You

needed to retain the integrity and grammar of the structure, the look and the feeling and detail, the way the house fit together." Yet the clients' changed needs also had to be met, within the spirit of the original design. "There was nothing that changed more than Taliesin," Olds stated. "Mr. Wright was constantly fine-tuning."[11]

The restoration of the Buehler House took about one year, from late 1995 to late 1996. The living room with its gold-leaf ceiling was rebuilt. Olds restored the ceiling in the dining room, where he applied a gold-leaf surface to the coffered panels Wright had designed, and installed new copper tracks to fit inside the

ABOVE: Buehler House, shop wing. FACING: Buehler House, master bedroom.

coffers and hold tiny bulbs that would highlight the gold leaf. A new copper roof was put on, the radiant heating was upgraded, and the walls were insulated with aluminum backing. The foundation had slipped about one and a half inches since 1949, so Olds had 13 new concrete piers sunk into the ground along the east side, which was closest to the nearby creek. A new skylight was installed in the master bedroom, and the third bedroom was converted into a dressing room to create a master suite. The skylight in the kitchen and the flashing around the chimney were made more water resistant (though some leaking still occurred until a more recent fix), and the kitchen was updated while retaining the basic contours and features of Wright's design. Maynard Buehler wanted to preserve as much of Wright's detail as possible, so when he realized that the new slab floor panels being laid down did not have the same groove as the originals, he raced to his workshop and created a trowel with the exact shape as the original grooves for the workers to use.[12]

Maynard died in 2005, and Katherine passed away in 2010. They had designated a close friend, Bob Ray, to be the executor of their estate. Since one of their daughters was deceased and the other didn't want to keep the house, Ray carried out some final upgrades and improvements before putting the house on the market in 2012. A new metal gate with a Wright-inspired decorative motif was created and installed across the driveway in front of the carport (most Usonian homes had carports instead of garages, one of Wright's many cost-saving features). The guesthouse and garden gazebo had new roofs put on. In the living room, Ray had mahogany caps placed over the old redwood armrests along the window seats to meet new code requirements. He also had the leaks around the kitchen skylight and the chimney fixed with a new sealant.[13] The Buehler House sold in December 2013 to a private owner, who will be enjoying a rare piece of Frank Lloyd Wright's remarkable legacy, a unique Usonian that was a source of peace and happiness for the original owners for six decades.

CHAPTER 6

FROM CARMEL TO THE CENTRAL VALLEY
Other Northern California Houses

"I wish protection from the wind and privacy from the road and a house as enduring as the rocks, but as transparent and charming as the waves and as delicate as a sea shore."

— Della Brooks Walker, in a letter to Frank Lloyd Wright, 1945

During the 50 years Frank Lloyd Wright was designing buildings in California, he spent much more time in Southern California than Northern California. In fact, Wright moved his office to Los Angeles in 1923, and lived in that city for the next two years before moving back to the Midwest (see Chapter 2). However, he designed a total of seven houses and three public buildings in Northern California between 1936 and 1959. Wright also had an office in San Francisco from the late 1940s through the late 1950s, during the time he was designing the V. C. Morris Gift Shop and later the Marin County Civic Center. During those years he often spent a few weeks at a time staying at hotels in San Francisco, and occasionally with clients who were also friends. Though he once disparagingly described San Francisco as "a city made of shanties," there is plenty of evidence from letters and interviews that he actually liked the City by the Bay, as well as the rest of Northern California.[1] He also occasionally had kind words for some local architects, such as Gardner Dailey and William Wurster, although he never praised the region's most respected architect, Bernard Maybeck, for whom he seemed to feel a keen sense of rivalry.[2]

Two of the clients with whom Wright became good friends were Professor Paul Hanna and his wife, Jean. This couple became his first Northern California clients when they commissioned a four-bedroom, proto-Usonian-style house from him on the campus of Stanford University in 1936. The Hanna House, nicknamed

"Honeycomb House" due to Wright's use of a repeated hexagonal pattern in his design of the floor plan, stands today in a quiet, tree-shaded corner of the Stanford campus known as "faculty ghetto." Except for some remodeling done by Wright for the Hannas in the 1950s, this 2,500-square-foot house has retained almost all of the original details and design features it had when it was completed in 1938.

Jean and Paul Hanna decided they wanted Frank Lloyd Wright to design a home for their family after reading some of Wright's lectures on architecture and visiting him at Taliesin East. They approached him about the project in 1936, stipulating that they wanted separate bedrooms for their three children, and that their total budget was only $15,000.[3] Wright had just completed his first Usonian house in Wisconsin, and he welcomed the opportunity to use this new design philosophy on a residence in California. The house he created for the Hanna family is actually a melding of some Prairie elements with primarily Usonian design features. Its Prairie elements consist of the mostly low-angled rooflines, wide overhanging eaves around all the exterior walls, and an overall horizontal massing. The Usonian features are the repeated hexagonal pattern in the floor plan, the modular units of wood paneling along the outside, and the prow-like gables set into the living room and dining room roofs.

Wright sited the Hanna House to take fullest possible advantage of the heavily wooded, parklike setting. The house sits atop a small knoll, which commands views of the rolling hillsides studded with valley oak and coast live oak trees that surround it. When

FACING: Walker House, Carmel, California (1948–54), detail of south side.

Above: Hanna House (Honeycomb House), Stanford, California (1936), northwest corner. Facing: Hanna House, west façade.

the house was being built, there were almost no other buildings visible in this part of the 8,180-acre Stanford campus.[4] In keeping with his organic design philosophy, he incorporated a 60-year-old Monterey cypress on the lot into his plans by putting an opening for it in the roof that adjoins the two carports at the northern end of the house. Wright also left a 200-year-old valley oak at the south end, letting its broad overhanging branches shade the children's playroom (it was later converted to a dining room).[5] The wide overhanging eaves provide shade from the California sun for all the other rooms in the house (in Wright's plans, he called the eaves "trellises"). The front entrance to the house is at the north end. The small doorway has a low clearance, which opens into a compact, narrow entry hall. When one walks into the living

room on the right, the ceiling is much higher and the effect of the open, spacious floor plan creates a very dramatic contrast, a classic example of Wright's technique of compression and release that he employed in so many of his residences.

The honeycomb, or hexagonal, pattern of the floor plan is evident upon entering the large, bright living room, which flows into the dining room at the southern end of the house. The rooms are arranged along a series of adjoining diagonal lines, with the living room wrapping around the centrally located fireplace, with its red brick, floor-to-ceiling facing. Four shallow concrete steps lead up to the dining room. Both rooms have concrete slab floors in Cherokee red with hexagonal patterns scored into them. The western walls of these rooms consist of floor-to-ceiling horizontal panes of glass, framed by California redwood, as are the built-in seats around the fireplace and the rear wall of the dining room, as well as the built-in bookcases in the living room. The combination of the redwood-framed windows and built-ins, the red concrete floors, and the massive red brick fireplace create a warm, inviting ambience, one that Wright continued throughout the rest of the house. Perhaps the most striking feature of the Hanna House is the sense of being surrounded by the natural beauty of the wooded hillsides, which are easily seen through the walls of horizontal windowpanes. This feature is a classic example of the indoor-outdoor effect Wright used on all his best residences, from his earliest Prairie-style homes in the early 1900s to his late Usonian houses in the 1950s.

The kitchen of the Hanna House, as in most of his later Usonian homes, is tucked into a space behind the living room fireplace wall, and it opens onto the current dining room (in the original floor plan, a small alcove between the living room and the playroom served as the dining room). For the first 20 years the Hannas lived here, it had four bedrooms along the eastern, or back, side of the house: one bedroom for each of their three children and a master bedroom. There were two full baths, and

a "sanctum," or study, for Paul. Wright also designed a servants' quarters and attached guesthouse beyond the carports, but these were not built until the 1950s.[6]

Construction on the house began in early January 1937, and letters between the Hannas and Mr. Wright show that the Hannas were closely involved in the refinements and final changes to Wright's original plans. Paul Hanna had carpentry skills, and he and Wright developed a friendly relationship, one based on mutual respect and common interests. The Hannas and Wright shared an interest in music and literature, and they remained friends for the rest of their lives. That is not to say there was never any tension between Wright and his clients, as there often was in many of his other important commissions. One example of this is a letter from Wright to Paul and Jean, which was in response to some concerns they had over his rigid adherence to the modular floor plan and the tight dimensions this would impose on features like the bathrooms and doorways. Wright's response, which was included in the Hanna's personal account of the project, titled *Frank Lloyd Wright's Hanna House: The Client's Report,* was dated January 27, 1937, and displays some of the sarcastic wit for which he was famous:

I am afraid the full import of the plans for your domicile hasn't yet penetrated your scholarly brain, and that reality has yet to dawn there. For instance: I've tried to impress upon you the fact that stock and shop proportions in planning modern houses were as clumsy and wasteful as they were ugly. Conservation of space based upon the proportions of the human figure has taken place actually, so far as I know, only in building ships and Pullman cars, the Imperial Hotel, and my own houses, although "modern architecture" had done something.

This house of yours is the latest essay in that direction wherein good aesthetics call for adequate but economic treatment of this important matter where living in houses is concerned. . . . Now indubitably, when the proportions of doors and furnishings are measured by the simple requirements of human use, there is greater satisfaction in the freedom to use the whole space. The house seems larger—the rooms seem and are larger while, certainly, physical comfort is no less. Briefly, this is the thesis. You have heard it from me before. And I am sure when you concentrate on it without too much ring around the rosie and holding of outside hands you will recognize its common sense. Or shall we say science? It is the kind of science that is the true basis for art.

After you have in hand the drawings we have been making to extra illustrate the plans (which will be very soon now) and our builder has digested them, if you feel it is necessary, I will send a superintendent to stay with you while you need him. I don't want to promise anything about my own advent. Whatever gods may be take umbrage where there is too much presumption. I hope this lets in light and restores confidence. If it does not, why then let those same gods have mercy.[7]

Paul and Jean made it quite clear in the comments in their account that they did not find offense with Wright's comments, but saw them as good-natured ribbing. Wright reassured them on more than one occasion that he was their "protection," and he would make certain they would get the home they wanted. Construction on the Hanna House was completed in the fall of 1937, and Paul and Jean and their three children moved into their new home in late November, just in time for Thanksgiving. After four months of finishing work on interior details, the Hannas invited Wright to come visit them. He showed up on April 4, 1938, along with 20 of his apprentices, to stay for the weekend. He had not seen the house since before it had been completed. When he entered the living room, he stood there for a moment looking around admiringly, and finally said,

Hanna House, dining room looking north.

1938. Picnic with family and friends

Paul and Jean Hanna (couple on left), family picnic at their house, c. 1938. Courtesy of Hanna House Collection, sc0280. Department of Special Collections & University Archives, Stanford University Libraries, Stanford, California.

1937. This is a home?

Jean Hanna in living room of her house, c. 1937. Courtesy of Hanna House Collection, sc0280. Department of Special Collections & University Archives, Stanford University Libraries, Stanford, California.

FACING, BOTTOM: Hanna House, dining room looking south. ABOVE: Hanna House, living room. RIGHT: Hanna House, detail of fireplace.

ABOVE: Hanna House, kitchen. RIGHT: Hanna House, master bedroom.

"Why, it's more beautiful than I had imagined; we have created a symphony here."[8] The final cost of the original house, including preparing the hillside lot for construction, came to $39,000.[9]

After living in the house for several years, the Hannas decided they needed to add on to the original home to accommodate the increased number of guests they were hosting, as well as create a woodworking shop. They hired Wright to draw new plans for these additions, and after several unforeseen delays, construction on the new wing began in late April 1950. The new wing was off the carports, at the northern end of their property. The work was finished on time, three months later. Again, in 1957, after their three children had moved out of the house, Paul and Jean decided to hire Wright to remodel the east side of the main house, since they didn't need four bedrooms anymore. He drew up plans to convert two of the children's bedrooms at the south end of the house into a large master bedroom and bath. He also converted the

middle bedroom into a TV room, as well as remodeling the two other rooms at the north end into a large library and study. This is the current floor plan of the house. Aaron Green was appointed by Wright to supervise all of the final remodeling, working from preliminary plans drawn by Wright.

Other changes were made to the lot during the nearly 40 years that the Hannas occupied the home. A circular driveway from Frenchmans Road was created in the late 1940s by Wright's studio. A freestanding teahouse was constructed in the 1960s, designed by Wes Peters from Taliesin Associated Architects. Peters also supervised construction of the cascading water feature in the backyard, which Wright designed for the Hannas in the 1930s but they decided not to build until 1961.[10] In the front yard the Hannas placed a massive carved stone lantern they brought from the Wright-designed Imperial Hotel in Tokyo, which was salvaged when that building was torn down in 1967.

Hanna House, library.

During the 1960s, Paul and Jean began planning for the future of their home. They wanted it to be preserved and serve a useful purpose after they were gone. In 1975 they moved out of the house, after Stanford University decided it would maintain the house as a residence for the university provost. In December 1976, after lobbying of various corporate donors by the Hannas for funds to preserve the house, Frank Lloyd Wright's reputation in Japan proved fruitful in the form of an endowment by the Nissan Motor Company to maintain and preserve the Hanna House and its grounds. Between 1979 and 1989 four provosts lived there.[11] In 1989 the Loma Prieta earthquake did serious damage to the house, making it unsafe to inhabit for a while. Condoleezza Rice, who became the university provost in 1993, agreed to authorize the $1.8 million in repairs the home needed.[12] After the restoration was completed in 1999, the house was opened to the public for tours by appointment. Hanna House was placed on the National Register of Historic Places in 1978.

▼ ▼ ▼ ▼ ▼

After the Hanna House, Wright designed two other houses on the peninsula south of San Francisco. The first one was for Sidney Bazett in 1938, at 101 Reservoir Road in Hillsborough. The rear of this house embraces a private elevated meadow, and it stands exactly as it appeared after Wright designed an addition in 1954. Hillsborough is a wealthy, secluded community of substantial homes on large lots. The Bazett House is an exception to this, with a total of only 2,046 square feet, including the addition. Wright

Bazett House, Hillsborough, California (1938), entry exterior.

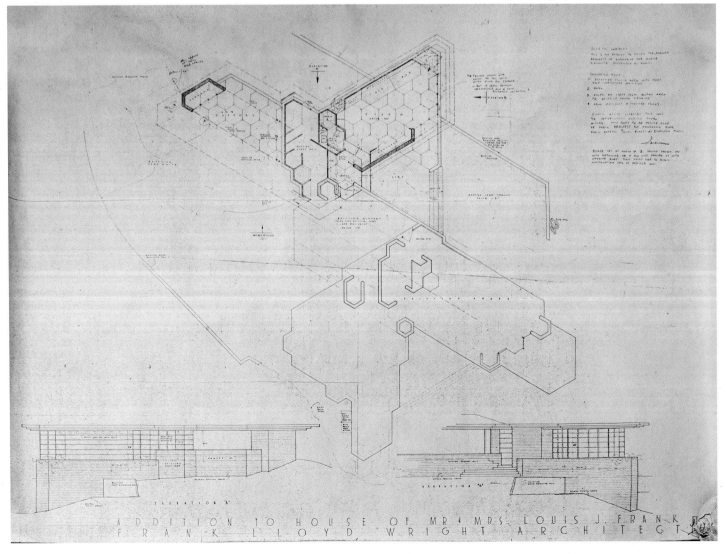

ABOVE: Bazett
House, east façade.
LEFT: Bazett
House, blueprint
of elevation A
and B with floor
plan. Copyright ©
The Frank Lloyd
Wright Foundation,
Scottsdale, Arizona.
FACING: Bazett
House, living room.

employed the same hexagonal version of the Usonian-style floor plan here that he had used on the Hanna House.

The Bazett House is a V-shaped, single-story residence, with walls made of red brick on the lower portions and laminated redwood on the upper sections. The living room wing has an unusual, undulating façade on the wall facing the meadow. Wright used the same horizontal, wood-latticed, floor-to-ceiling windows on this wall that he used on the Hanna House. The roof is low-angled, with a gently sloping overhanging gable at the end of the living room wing. Flat overhanging eaves continue around the rest of the exterior. A massive brick chimney rises above the intersection of the two wings, and the roof above the bedroom wing is flat. There is a brick terrace around the perimeter of the main house. Wright placed a carport between the main house and the guest wing he designed beside it. A covered walkway leads to the entrance to this detached guest wing, which has its own small terrace behind the carport.

The living room of the Bazett House, like many other Usonian homes, has a high ceiling that rises to a peak in the center. The solid redwood front door is almost hidden, tucked beneath the overhang on the north side. After the low entryway, one enters into the grand space of the living room, a classic example of Wright's dramatic compression-and-release technique. The ceiling here is wood paneled, as are the main walls. Indirect lighting brightens the space above the west wall, where Wright placed a long alcove lined with low built-in seating and bookshelves. A geometric pattern in sawn wood graces the clerestory along the top of this alcove. At the far end of the living room, a magnificent set of undulating floor-to-ceiling windows open out onto the terrace and flood the room with natural light. Wright placed a brick-faced fireplace at the opposite end of

the room. The living room flows into an open dining area, and a small, enclosed kitchen with a skylight sits at the apex of the two wings. The bedrooms are in the south wing, which has lower wood-paneled ceilings that are flat. This creates the impression of a series of small cabin-like rooms, but the rich wood paneling along the walls gives these bedrooms warmth, and the floor-to-ceiling windows provide ample light.

Construction of the Bazett House was completed in 1940. In 1945, Betty and Lou Frank bought the house, and they soon decided they needed more space for their children. In the mid-1950s, they asked Wright to expand the guest wing, so he added a playroom to the guest bedroom for their boys to use. This space was later converted into a studio and adjacent bedroom after the boys moved out. In a

FACING: Bazett House, view from entryway to living room. RIGHT, TOP: Bazett House, north end. RIGHT, BOTTOM: Bazett House, view from living room towards kitchen.

testament to the pleasant ambience of the Bazett House, the famed California midcentury architect Joseph Eichler rented it for a while just before the Franks bought it. Eichler loved the house so much that he tried to prevent the sale to the Franks from going through. Years later, when he had established his own very successful practice, he attributed his inspiration for his light-filled home designs to the experience of living in the Bazett House.

▼ ▼ ▼ ▼ ▼

Ten miles south of the Bazett House stands the Arthur C. Mathews House, at 83 Wisteria Way in the leafy, tony suburb of Atherton, designed by Wright in 1950 and constructed the same year. The Mathews House is an individualized example of a late Usonian house, one that is based on paired, four-by-four-foot equilateral triangles, which create a diamond pattern for the floor plan. The two wings extend from the central work area and dining space.

BELOW: Mathews House, Atherton, California (1950), detail of entryway.
RIGHT: Mathews House, west façade. Photographs © 1988 Scot Zimmerman.

The living room wing is at a 120-degree angle to the workspace, while the bedroom wing is at a 60-degree angle. There are three bedrooms and two bathrooms in this modest-sized home.

The exterior walls are mostly composed of floor-to-ceiling windows with wide sections of red brick in between—similar to the walls in the Bazett House, but with an even greater portion given

to not install any of Wright's built-in furniture.

▼ ▼ ▼ ▼ ▼

Frank Lloyd Wright often extolled the virtues of having his clients build their own homes from a set of his plans. One of the most important aspects of his Usonian concept was that the structures were both simple enough and affordable enough for the average, educated homebuilder to be their own contractor, when they had the required skills (although in practice these homes did not always prove to be simple or inexpensive to construct, as we have seen from earlier examples). Perhaps the ultimate example of an entirely owner-built home done from Wright's plans is the Robert Berger House in the quiet, upscale Marin County community of San Anselmo.

In 1950, Robert and Gloria Berger purchased a one-acre, tree-studded lot at the top of a hill, at 259 Redwood Road in San Anselmo. Their lot had a panoramic view of the verdant, rolling hills and valleys surrounding it. While deciding on how to proceed with building a home for

over to glass. These "walls of windows" create a seamless flow from indoor to outdoor spaces. The two wings embrace a semiprivate terrace and large lawn. The roof is a low-angled hipped roof made of wood shingles with wide overhanging eaves. The interior is finished in board-and-batten redwood paneling. This is one of the few Wright-designed homes where the owner-builder decided

themselves and their three children, they saw an article on Wright's V. C. Morris Gift Shop in San Francisco in *Architectural Forum*. The shop had just been finished, and the article mentioned that Wright was currently working out of his San Francisco office. So Robert wrote a letter to Mr. Wright, asking him to design a two-bedroom house for his family. In a 1959 article in *Life* magazine, the author

ABOVE: Berger House, San Anselmo, California (1950–58), Robert Berger building masonry core, c. 1955. Courtesy of Berger Family Collection. RIGHT, TOP: Berger House, south façade. RIGHT, BOTTOM: Berger House, floor plan. Copyright © The Frank Lloyd Wright Foundation, Scottsdale, Arizona. FACING: Berger House, blueprint of north, south, east, and west elevations. Copyright © The Frank Lloyd Wright Foundation, Scottsdale, Arizona.

explained: "Over his wife's objections that he was crazy and that surely Mr. Wright would scorn a do-it-yourself project, he wrote to the famous architect. Wright replied by asking for his lot size and a description of his property. In a few months he sent the plans along."[13] The plans were ready by the fall of 1950, but construction was delayed by Robert's military service in the Korean War. When Robert returned from the war in 1952, he got a job teaching math at Novato High School, and then at the College of Marin. He decided the time was right to begin construction on his home.

Over the next six years, Robert Berger worked on the house mostly by himself, although Aaron Green acted as consulting architect on the project. His wife, Gloria, and occasionally their children, helped him with a number of tasks, including the plumbing, digging the foundation, and pouring concrete. The biggest task they worked on, and one of the first things to be completed, was building the 20-foot-tall fireplace shaft, which was the masonry core of the house. This required pouring 50 tons of rock and cement into a wooden mold, and it took several months to complete.[14] Robert created the distinct inlaid stone patterns on all the exterior walls out of local pink Sonoma stone (Wright called this material "desert masonry"). He gathered, chiseled, and fitted each of the several hundred stones into the walls by hand. His work had progressed enough by 1956 for the family to move into the first section of the house. The remaining section of the home, and all of the interior finishing work, was finally completed in 1958.[15]

The Berger House retains almost all of its original features, and is considered a gem of the Usonian style. It is a single-story, two-bedroom, two-bath home, with 1,760 square feet of living space and a built-in carport under the overhanging roof to the left of the front door. The low-angled hipped roof, the horizontal massing of the house, and the native stone walls make it appear to be a natural outgrowth of the forested hillside it sits atop. Wright designed the house on an equilateral parallelogram pattern, creating a hexagonal living room that juts off the north side of the home. The living room ceiling is higher than the other rooms, a typical feature of Usonian houses. There is a serene view of

ABOVE: Berger House, south façade. BELOW: Berger House, desert masonry with overhanging eaves. FACING: Berger House, dining room with Frank Lloyd Wright–designed built-in table.

the lushly wooded Marin hills in three directions from the floor-to-ceiling windows in the living room. A sliding glass door leads from the living room out onto the concrete deck, which is shaped like a ship's prow and points almost due north.

The other interior features of the Berger House display classic Usonian elements. The kitchen is in an alcove behind the living room, and there is a raised-hearth fireplace set into the rear wall of the living room, made of concrete inlaid with pink Sonoma stone. There are built-in shelves and cabinets in the kitchen, and one section of these shelves and cabinets runs out into the living room. A built-in table of mahogany extends off these shelves, creating a small dining area at the west end of the living room. Behind these shelves is a playroom for the Berger children, which could double as a study after they went to bed. This open-ended space has a built-in desk and bookshelves along the walls. There are also built-in window seats of redwood along two of the living room walls. The floors throughout the house are made of concrete slabs, scored in a hexagonal pattern and stained Cherokee red. Wright designed many built-in cabinets lining the walls throughout the rest of the home, to insure plenty of indoor storage space.

The original master bedroom and bath were directly behind the rear wall of the kitchen. This bedroom has been converted into a study, but it retains all its Wright-designed built-in bookshelves, cabinets, and nightstands. A gallery-style hallway

ABOVE: Berger House, living room. FACING: Walker House, Carmel, California (1948–54), south view.

leads from the east end of the living room to the rest of the living quarters. The hallway has more built-in storage cabinets along its walls. The second and third bedrooms are off the eastern end of this hallway, with a bathroom tucked in between them. There is a built-in desk along one wall of the larger bedroom, so the children could do their homework there. A spacious workshop occupies the south-eastern corner of the house, accessible from the larger bedroom. The northern exterior wall of this wing rises about eight feet from the ground to the floor level and tapers inward, creating a battered wall effect, often used in Tibetan monasteries.

The front door to the Berger House is hidden underneath the wide overhanging eaves on the south side of the house. These eaves are embellished by a repeating cutout pattern along a frieze that lines the entire south side, much like the eaves on the Buehler House. There is a parking area for four cars in front of the carport, and a pink-stained concrete patio to the left of the front door. A low retaining wall made out of the same stone-embedded concrete as the house lines this patio on the south and west sides.

The Berger House remains structurally sound to this day, nearly 60 years after it was built. There is no sign of settling of the foundation or cracking on the floors, and there was no noticeable damage from the 1989 Loma Prieta earthquake. Thus, the solid condition of this "do-it-yourself" Frank Lloyd Wright–designed home is a rebuke to those critics who claim that Wright's houses were not well engineered.

▼ ▼ ▼ ▼ ▼

In the 1959 Hollywood film *A Summer Place,* a middle-aged couple invites their two grown children to stay with them in their new beachfront home, supposedly on the Atlantic Coast. The house that was actually used for this scene was the Mrs. Clinton Walker House in Carmel, California, just south of Monterey Bay. As the wife opens the door to their house, she proudly says, "Frank Lloyd Wright designed our house." But when they go inside, the interior bears no resemblance to Wright's design. A set was used instead, making the house appear to be two stories, and much more spacious than it really is.

The actual Walker House is one of Frank Lloyd Wright's most popular designs with the general public. Besides being used as a setting in the above-mentioned film, the exterior of the home has been photographed by hundreds of thousands of tourists over the nearly

six decades since its completion. It was also one of Wright's favorite residential commissions, one that he referred to as a little masterpiece appropriate to the unique site. The reason both Wright and his client were so pleased with this design is obvious to anyone who has stood on the beach at Carmel and looked up at the Walker House perched comfortably atop its prominent outcropping, overlooking the deep blue waters and massive rocks of Carmel Bay. The Walker House is a perfect blending of nature and building; of sea, sky, sand, and stone—and of local materials with the magnificent natural setting. In short, it is a masterful example of Wright's philosophy of organic design, flawlessly executed. The process of designing and building this house, however, was anything but seamless, as a number of testy exchanges between Mrs. Walker and Wright during the construction of her residence make abundantly clear.

The genesis of the Walker House dates back to 1945, when Clinton Walker's widow, Della Brooks Walker, purchased a one-acre lot on a prominent outcropping along Carmel Bay. She wrote a letter to Frank Lloyd Wright on June 13, 1945, describing her site and asking if he would design a beachfront house for her:

LEFT: Walker House, view toward the bay. BELOW: Della Walker in living room of her house, c. 1952. Courtesy of Walker Family Collection. RIGHT: Walker House, view of windows along south side.

I own a rocky point of land in Carmel, California extending into the Pacific Ocean. The surface is flat, and it is located at the end of a white sand beach. I am a woman living alone. I wish protection from the wind and privacy from the road and a house as enduring as the rocks, but as transparent and charming as the waves and as delicate as a sea shore. You are the only man who can do this— will you help me?[16]

Before she decided to write this letter, Mrs. Walker said to her friends and family that the reason she chose Wright as her architect was because of his design for Fallingwater. "If he could do that for a stream," her great-grandson quotes her as saying, "just imagine what he could do with an ocean?"[17] Obviously, Mrs. Walker was a woman who knew exactly what she wanted, and who knew how to express herself clearly and eloquently to get it.

When Wright received Mrs. Walker's letter, he responded promptly, saying he'd be happy to design her house. There were delays in the starting of the project, however, due to Wright's work on other buildings. Construction finally began in April 1948, but a shortage of building materials during the Korean War interrupted the project once more. The house was finally completed in November 1952, and Mrs. Walker lived there alone for the next 26 years, until her death in 1978.

The Walker House is a single-story, five-room residence with three bedrooms, a combination living room/dining room, a small kitchen, and a total of 1,200 square feet of living space. The back bedroom was enlarged in the early 1960s from drawings done by Wright and executed by Sandy Walker, Della Walker's grandson.[18] This is not a typical Usonian house, but rather a unique example of Wright's organic design principles, a gem he created to fit perfectly into its natural setting through the integration of the structure and materials with its site. The fact that this was one of Wright's favorite residences out of all his West Coast work is clearly indicated by the fact that in his correspondence with Mrs. Walker during and after the construction, he affectionately referred to it as the "Cabin on the Rocks," and called it "a little masterpiece."[19]

The living room/dining room faces due west, and is the most impressive room in the house, with its sweeping vista of Carmel Bay, the white sand beaches that line it, and the blue waters of the Pacific Ocean beyond. The tiers of metal-framed windows that encircle this room are slanted outward, to reduce the glare from the sunlight on the water in the late afternoon. The wide, overhanging eaves of the low-hipped roof also serve to reduce glare. The roof was originally clad in blue green porcelain to reflect the colors of the ocean. However, as with so many other Wright homes, this roof began leaking soon after construction was completed, so it was replaced with a copper roof about 1960.

The living room is designed in a four-by-four-foot parallelogram pattern, which was used for the entire floor plan. The west front of the house forms a prow-like projection, as does the terrace running in front of the living room, which is made out of concrete faced with

BELOW: Walker House, view of living room windows. FACING: Walker House, view of living room with fireplace.

Carmel stone. The prominent prow shapes of these features, pointing out to sea, create an impression of a ship about to be launched into the ocean. Wright placed a row of window seats all along the west end of the living room, to make it easier for the residents to enjoy the view. He also designed a small dining table made from triangular sections (the current chairs were also designed by Wright, but are replacements that were added later). The open-hearth fireplace that forms the rear wall of the living room is faced in Carmel stone. When it was first installed, the stones were incorrectly set in a horizontal pattern. So Aaron Green, the supervising architect, told the contractors to take them out and reinstall them with an upward slant as Wright had intended. The living room ceiling tilts upward from the edges toward the center, and is made of combed plywood.

The walls throughout the house are made of cedar panels with beveled battens, and the floors are made of concrete slabs, scored in a four-by-four-foot parallelogram pattern and stained Cherokee red.

A gallery-style hallway runs along the south side of the house, which is sheltered from the glare of the afternoon sun by custom-designed blinds with thin slats that tilt at just the right angle to allow views of the beach and still provide shade. The small front door is at the west end of the hallway. Two bedrooms and two full baths open onto the hallway. The enlarged master suite in the rear wing has a large adjoining bath and a big fireplace lined in Carmel stone along the north wall. This bedroom opens onto a spacious trapezoidal deck along the north side of the house, which has unobstructed views of the beach and the ocean below.

Before construction on the Walker House was completed, a request from Della Walker about the kitchen caused a battle royal with Mr. Wright. She wanted a door put into the north wall of the kitchen so she could put the trash can out easily. In a testy letter dated February 27, 1951, Wright stated his strenuous objection:

> *Again we are up in the air—Looks very much as though the Cabin on the Rocks was on the rocks in more than one sense. You were once of my mind about the cabin. You gave me reason to think so, and I was happy to build it as I put my best mind and heart into producing a little masterpiece appropriate to the unique site. An ordinary little "door and window" house on that site would look as foolish as a hen resting where you ought to see a seagull. I am unwilling to spoil my charming seabird and substitute the hen. You don't need me for that. Anyone can do it.[20]*

FACING: Walker House, kitchen. ABOVE: Walker House, detail of bathroom. BELOW: Walker House, master bedroom.

Wright and Mrs. Walker arrived at a compromise—to sink the trash can into a hole bored into the concrete deck so it couldn't be seen by passersby, thus removing one of Wright's concerns. He still opposed putting a door in the kitchen wall, but since *she* was paying the contractors, in the end she got her door. There were more testy exchanges between Mrs. Walker and Mr. Wright when construction was nearly complete. Della hired the renowned landscape architect Thomas Church to design the landscape scheme for the exterior of her house. When some of Wright's staff informed him of this, Wright again fired off an indignant letter of protest, dated March 21, 1952:

> *Distressing news from several quarters. One of my former apprentices says to Aaron Green "Someone has ruined Mr. Wright's house with landscaping. Walter Olds, distressed, said "Mrs. Walker hired a professional landscaper to undo all Mr. Wright has done for her." If you did employ one, it is the first time it has happened to me in a long lifetime of building. The first destructive insult. I don't believe it.*
>
> *Throughout the nation, these destructive vermin plant a skirt of shrubbery around a house and stick up a couple of trees at the entrance. A "William Worse than Wurster" might be benefitted by this stock performance. Not so the Cabin on the Rocks. Is it all true?—I hope what I hear is not true and loves labor lost. I love the Cabin and had it in my heart as well as my head.[21]*

But Mrs. Walker stuck to her guns, and once again her desires prevailed over the heated objections of Mr. Wright. Thomas Church's landscaping design was carried out largely as he had planned it, with no discernable detriment to the aesthetic effect of Wright's creation. Anyone who has strolled along the white sand beaches of Carmel and looked up to see the Walker House, set so perfectly into its rocky outcropping, would be happy to agree with Wright that the

Walker House, south façade.

Walton House, Modesto, California (1957–61), view of west façade.

Cabin on the Rocks is indeed a little masterpiece that fits beautifully into its unique site.

▼ ▼ ▼ ▼ ▼

On the outskirts of Modesto in the heart of the Central Valley, on a 10-acre lot studded with old almond trees, sits one of the most unusual Frank Lloyd Wright houses on the West Coast. The Robert G. Walton House, at 417 Hogue Road, is one of Wright's largest residences of the 1950s. This 3,200-square-foot, single-story house is a modified version of Wright's Usonian-style homes. Many of its features are not Usonian at all, but the result of the original owners, Robert and Mary Walton, insisting on full input into the design of their home, and convincing Mr. Wright to accept their ideas—no small feat, as we have seen. At this writing, Robert and Mary Walton still own and occupy this house, and it retains nearly all of its original features.

Mary Walton first met Frank Lloyd Wright at Taliesin East in the late 1940s, when she was in her teens. She went there because her brother, Douglas Lee, was working at Taliesin as an intern. She and her mother had dinner there, and heard Wright speak about architecture. Growing up in Michigan, Mary had seen several Frank Lloyd Wright houses, and decided she wanted him to design one for her when she got married. In 1955, a few years after she married British-born dermatologist Robert Walton, they bought a level lot in a rural tract that had been an almond orchard, about a half mile south of the Stanislaus River. The lot still has many old almond trees along its western edge, as well as several 400-year-old valley oaks shading its eastern and northern sides. The site retains the feeling of being completely out in the country.

Soon after they purchased their lot, Mary wrote a letter to Wright, asking him to design a home for them. He agreed, and they went to visit him at Taliesin West in 1957. During a detailed conversation with them about the design of their house, Mary

ABOVE, LEFT: Walton House, view down walkway to front door. ABOVE, RIGHT: Walton House, view of east side with pool. BELOW: Walton House, blueprint of general plan. Copyright © The Frank Lloyd Wright Foundation, Scottsdale, Arizona.

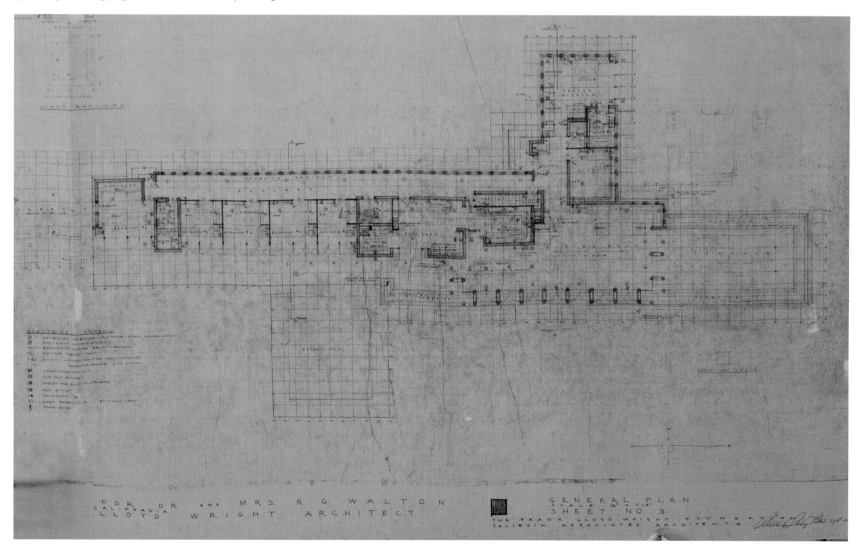

LEFT: Walton House, view of south terrace looking through living room.

Walton House, living room.

suggested building it out of adobe bricks, to fit in with the local Spanish Colonial–style architecture. Ignoring her, Wright turned to her husband and announced, "Dr. Walton, I build scientific houses out of concrete block and steel reinforcement, so I know that they are safe." Dr. Walton replied, "Yes, Mr. Wright," and agreed to build their home of those materials.[22] Wright's bid for the project was $60,000, and surprisingly the final cost actually came to very nearly that amount.

Once construction began in early 1958, however, the Waltons would request, and obtain, a number of modifications of Wright's

ABOVE: Mary Walton, 2010. Courtesy of Walton Family Collection.
FACING: Walton House, gallery.

original plans. The house took nearly one year to complete, and they moved in just before Christmas 1958. Wes Peters was their supervising architect, and although Wright never visited the site, the Waltons had regular communication with him during construction. Wright's design was a six-bedroom house along a north–south axis, with a living room, a dining room, a kitchen, a playroom, two studies, three and a half baths, and a two-car carport at the south end.

The floor plan of the Walton House forms a long "L" shape, with a short tail at the northern end. The exterior walls are made of concrete blocks, painted a light pink salmon color. The roof is

flat, except for a squared ventilation tower that rises over the kitchen (which Mary Walton calls "our Norman tower"). Most of the wall area along the eastern façade is taken up with floor-to-ceiling banded picture windows, and the western façade has a clerestory of windows above the built-in shelving along the inside. A concrete slab terrace runs around the west, south, and north sides of the house, stained Cherokee red. A long patio runs off the north end of the house, accessible from the living room through tall glass doors. There is a swimming pool set into the east terrace. Wright's original plan called for a rectangular pool, but Mary's brother redesigned it as a nonrectangular parallelogram and installed it three years later.

The front entrance to the house is on the south side of the west wing. The interior was designed in a modified Usonian style, based on a 32-inch-square grid pattern for the floor plan. To the left as you enter is a large study and a master bedroom suite with one of the most spacious bathrooms in any of Wright's California Usonian residences. To the right is the light-filled living room, with floor-to-ceiling banded windows and doors on the north and east sides. These doors and windows are framed in Philippine mahogany, as are the built-in cabinets below the wall of windows along the eastern side, and the built-in bookshelves along the western wall. There is an open-hearth fireplace on the south wall. Several original Wright-designed straight-backed chairs are still used by the Waltons in this living room, as are the Wright-designed chairs in the adjacent formal dining room.

A formal dining room is a rarity in a Usonian house, but the Waltons insisted on having one. This room can be closed off by using the Pella folding doors that Mary asked Wright to install. The ceilings in both the living and dining rooms are 12 feet high, another unusual feature in a Wright-designed residence that the Waltons were able to get Mr. Wright to agree to. Robert also asked to have a built-in wet bar in the living room, but Wright recommended a portable one. Robert insisted, and Wright finally acquiesced. To the right of the dining room is the galley-style kitchen, with much more cabinet space and workspace than most Usonian houses, a concession to Mary, as was the tall ventilation tower with a skylight set into the ceiling. A playroom was placed adjacent to the kitchen, which is now used as a small library.

Walton House, view of dining room.

Along the western side of the house is an 80-foot-long gallery-style hallway, which connects the five bedrooms in this wing of the house. A full bath sits between the fourth and fifth bedrooms. The shelves along the west wall of this hallway provide lots of storage space, and are enclosed by latched doors that open outward.

The Waltons also insisted that the heating and air conditioning for their home be air blown, instead of a radiant heating system from pipes set into the slab floor as was used in most Usonian houses. When Wright suggested that they didn't really need an air-blown air-conditioning system and could simply rely on crosscurrents from opening all the doors and windows to cool the house, Mary simply replied, "I'm sorry Mr. Wright, but when it's 108 degrees outside in the summer and there's no breeze, that just won't work."[23] So once again, Wright reluctantly agreed.

▼ ▼ ▼ ▼ ▼

Much has been written about the few homes that were designed by Frank Lloyd Wright before his death in 1959, but not built until after he died. Taliesin kept all of Wright's unbuilt plans, and a number of them were authorized to be used by the original clients later on, or new clients who wanted a Wright-designed home after the master's death. I have often jokingly referred to these houses as examples of Wright's "postmortem period." One such residence, which is perhaps the most accurate example of a

postmortem Wright design being executed exactly as he planned it, is the Hilary and Joe Feldman House in Berkeley, California.

The Feldman House stands in the Berkeley Hills above the UC Berkeley campus, at 13 Mosswood Road. It was originally designed in 1939 for Mr. and Mrs. Lewis N. Bell for a lot in the Hollywood Hills in Southern California. However, the Bells decided they couldn't afford the cost of construction, so the plans remained at Taliesin. Thirty-five years later, Berkeley tax attorney Joe Feldman was doing some work for Wright's widow, Olgivanna Wright, and she could not afford to pay his fee right away. So in lieu of payment, he arranged for permission to use the existing plans for the Bells' house to construct a residence on a pie-shaped lot he had bought in the Berkeley Hills. The plan had to be flip-flopped to fit conveniently into the new lot, and Olgivanna walked around the site before giving her approval for the project. Wright's original designs

Feldman House, Berkeley, California (1937–74), view along north terrace.

for the furniture and drapes were included as part of the agreement, which Joe was happy to accept as a precondition for Olgivanna's approval.[24]

Construction began on the Feldman House in 1974, and was completed in 1976. But by the time the house was completed, Feldman's wife, Hilary, had been offered a teaching position at Oxford University, and moved to England to accept this position. So Joe Feldman lived in the house by himself for only a few months while the house was on the market. He eventually moved to Oxford to be with his wife, and the house was finally sold in 1980 to Marc Grant and Jeanne Allen, who have lived in it ever since. They couldn't afford to buy the original furniture, so the Feldmans gave it to the Victoria and Albert Museum in London. After living in the house for nearly 30 years, Marc and Jeanne contacted a curator they knew at the Victoria and Albert and asked if they could have the furniture, since it had never been put on display. The museum said yes, and after inspecting the furniture in London, they were asked to pay only the shipping cost of having it sent to Berkeley, where it has been placed in the house since 2010, just as Wright had planned it.

The Feldman House is a 1,100-square-foot, single-story Usonian house with a total of five rooms: one bedroom, one bath, a study, a combination living room/dining room, and a kitchen. There is a very wide terrace around the entire perimeter of the house, with superb views of the city of Berkeley, and San Francisco Bay and the Golden Gate beyond. These views can also be seen from much of the interior due to Wright's placement of floor-to-ceiling plate glass windows all around the north, south, and west sides. This feature, together

Feldman House, living room with Frank Lloyd Wright–designed furniture.

with its prominent hilltop location, gives the Feldman House one of the lightest interiors of all of Wright's West Coast residences.

The spacious living room is accessed from the small front door on the north side of the house, after passing through a two-car carport and a red metal gate in a fence that Wright designed to surround the west and north perimeters of the tree-shaded lot. Upon entering the living room, the immediate impression is one of a light-filled, open, flowing space with walls of glass framed with redwood along three sides. The floors in the center of the room are made of oak, while those around the outer edges are made from concrete slabs stained Cherokee red. An open-hearth fireplace is set into the rear wall of the living room, with a built-in redwood sofa adjacent to it, and there are built-in redwood window seats along the north side. The ceiling here is higher than in many Usonian houses, and is made of

LEFT: Feldman House, view through terrace doors to living room. FACING: Feldman House, kitchen.

redwood plywood with geometric decorative trim, and has a raised section above the middle with a clerestory of cutout geometric patterns. The kitchen is hexagonal, and retains the original built-in shelves and butcher-block countertops.

The walls of the Feldman House are red brick facing over concrete block, giving the home an overall warm quality. The same materials were used for the retaining walls along the north, west, and south sides. The terrace that runs along these three sides has two-and-a-half-foot-high brick borders, lined with built-in redwood seating in several places, making this area perfect for outdoor dining and entertaining. The roof is flat, with wide overhanging eaves. Wright's original plans did not include a basement, but when Joe Feldman built the house he had a full basement dug out of the steep downslope lot. Other than this change, the Feldman House is a faithful incarnation of a Frank Lloyd Wright–designed home set into the Berkeley Hills—one that appears perfectly suited to its current location.

▼ ▼ ▼ ▼ ▼

In the tiny, rural community of Los Banos east of Interstate 5 in California's Central Valley sits one of Frank Lloyd Wright's most unusual houses, one with several innovative features that were years ahead of their time. The Randall Fawcett House, at 2120 Center Avenue, is a late Usonian House. It was designed in 1955, but the

BELOW: Fawcett House, Los Banos, California (1955–61), north façade with three-car carport. RIGHT: Fawcett House, south façade, c. 1980s. Photograph © 1988 Scot Zimmerman.

construction was carried out by Taliesin Associated Architects, and not completed until 1961.[25] Thus it could be considered another example of Wright's postmortem-period homes, like the Feldman House in Berkeley.

The Fawcett House is in the shape of a wide "U," which embraces an enclosed lush lawn and garden area. At the northeast corner of the house is a trapezoidal pool, bordered by a series of concrete steps and terraces. The overall effect of this setting is to create the impression of a desert oasis, where one can refresh body and soul after walking through the unrelenting heat of the Central Valley in summer. The walls of the house are made of concrete blocks, tapered inward. Another unusual feature is the low-angled roof, which is cantilevered out several feet over the walls. The edges of the roof are encased in metal sheathing with geometric patterns, and the overhangs are perforated with jagged, metal-framed holes that cast interesting patterns when the sun shines through onto the concrete terraces below. The private side of the house, facing the garden and pool, has walls made of floor-to-ceiling windows and doors. These walls are not load bearing, as Wright used steel I-beams within the cantilevered roof for support.

At the top of the wall leading to the front entrance of the Fawcett House, Wright placed a shallow urn-shaped flower box, similar to the one he used on the entry gate of the Walker House in Carmel. The front door is on the northwest façade, set well back beneath a wide overhang that provides shade from the hot sun. This opens into a spacious rectangular living room, which occupies most of the central wing. The dominant feature of this room is the wide walk-in fireplace set into the south wall. There is an inglenook flanking the fireplace, made from concrete footings. The wall along this side of the room slants outward, and the

BELOW: Fawcett House, detail of south façade. FACING: Fawcett House, living room. Photographs © 1988 Scot Zimmerman.

ceiling tilts slightly upward to the middle, then levels off. Wright placed triangular recesses along the midline of this ceiling, with hanging light fixtures in them. Along the upper walls of the living room, as well as the entry hall, Wright designed a clerestory with cutout geometric patterns, as he did in so many other Usonian houses. These clerestories are made out of cedar trim over Plexiglas. The floors throughout this house are made of the same concrete slabs found in other Usonians, but they are stained dark brown rather than the usual Cherokee red.

In the southwest wing of the Fawcett House, Wright placed four bedrooms and three baths, as well as the master bedroom suite at the end. The southeast wing contains the kitchen and a large playroom, with a built-in dining table attached at the north end. This long room opens out onto the pool. A three-car attached carport runs off the northeast corner of the house, with a tool shed at the far end. As with all his other Usonian houses, Wright designed built-in bookshelves and window seats for the living room, and built-in furniture in most of the other rooms.

Wright's original choice for the site of the Fawcett House was in an adjacent walnut grove. But the clients decided this setting would be too humid, so the site of their house was moved a short distance. With all of its sharp-edged rooflines, wide overhangs, tapering walls, and geometric patterns in jagged metal, the Fawcett House resembles a smaller-scale residential version of the work of such au courant architects as Frank Gehry, whose "starkitecture" designs have come to dominate public architecture in cities around the globe since 2000. Here, once again, Frank Lloyd Wright was several decades ahead of his time.

CHAPTER 7

A GIFT TO THESE GOLDEN HILLS
The Marin County Civic Center, 1957-69

*"In Marin County you have one of the most beautiful landscapes I have seen, and I am
proud to make the buildings of this county characteristic of the beauty of the county."*

— Frank Lloyd Wright in comments to a public meeting, 1957

The hills in the eastern part of Marin County take on a golden yellow hue for most of the year. Their soft, rounded contours, sprinkled with scrub brush and clusters of live oaks, rise and fall in gentle waves as they undulate across the landscape. This is the setting for the most distinctive government complex in the United States, and the only government project designed by Frank Lloyd Wright that was ever built. The story of how it came to be, and the heated controversy it created when Wright first proposed his design, is one of the most interesting stories in the history of American architecture.

By the late 1950s, Marin County had a population approaching 150,000 that was spread out across an area of 520 square miles. This sprawling, semiurban community was served by an antiquated courthouse in downtown San Rafael, with various county offices scattered around 12 locations. These facilities were overcrowded and out of date, and inadequate for serving the needs of a well-educated, twentieth-century population that was experiencing rapid growth. Between 1950 and 1960, Marin County's population nearly doubled, from 86,000 to 147,000.[1] The county's civic and business leaders began to call for a new government center to be built that would house all of the government's offices and services in one location. In 1953, the Marin County Board of Supervisors appointed a "Site Committee for a Civic Center" and began looking for a site in San Rafael, the county seat.[2]

On April 27, 1956, a site in the open hills just north of downtown

FACING: Marin County Civic Center, San Rafael, California, Administration Building (1957–62), view of interior third and fourth levels.

San Rafael and east of Highway 101 was chosen. It was a private ranch in an area known as Santa Venetia, which the county purchased for $426,000. A new Civic Center Committee was appointed and given the task of selecting an architect for the project. During the next year, the committee interviewed dozens of architects, and provided 26 of their names to the board of supervisors for screening. Among them were internationally famed Austrian architect Richard Neutra and Frank Lloyd Wright. In April 1957, four of the board's five supervisors heard Frank Lloyd Wright lecture at UC Berkeley, and met with him later at his San Francisco office. Wright suggested to them that their new civic center should reflect the unique personality of the county, and they were convinced that he was the right architect for the job. The committee then recommended unanimously to the board of supervisors that Wright be hired as the architect for the project. So on June 26, 1957, the board voted four to one to begin negotiations with Frank Lloyd Wright.[3] And that's when the troubles began.

San Rafael is an old California town, founded in 1850 by Yankee pioneers, whose first rustic homes were clustered around the grounds of the former Spanish Mission San Rafael Arcángel, which had been abandoned before the gold rush.[4] Hundreds of Victorian-era homes and commercial buildings line the streets surrounding its historic business district. The hills just to the north of central San Rafael remained largely undeveloped open land in the late 1950s. Most of the city's business and political leaders agreed that this was an ideal site for a new civic center.

The local government was in the hands of an "old boys' network" of all male politicians until the election of 1955, when a more progressive group took office. The new board consisted of four men and one woman, Vera Schultz. Schultz was an early advocate of women having an equal voice with men in local government. She had been elected to the Marin County Board of Supervisors in 1952, the first woman ever to serve on that body, and held her seat for a total of eight years, where she earned the title "First Lady of Marin." Schultz was the most ardent backer of Frank Lloyd Wright to be the architect of the new civic center. If not for her unwavering support and ironclad determination in the face of heated opposition, Wright's design would never have been built. She had the support of three of the men on the board. But the fourth, William Fusselman, together with his ally, County Clerk George Jones, did everything they could to prevent Wright from getting the commission.[5] They would come very close to succeeding, on more than one occasion, in their campaign to derail Wright's plans and force the board to pick another architect.

On July 18, 1957, Fusselman invited Richard Neutra to make a design presentation to the board of supervisors for possible selection as the architect for the civic center instead of Wright. Afterwards the board voted to reject Neutra's proposal and continue their negotiations with Wright. Fusselman's objections to the selection of Wright were based on several factors. First, he thought the board had not given adequate consideration to other architects, particularly firms from the Bay Area or Los Angeles. At the board meeting on June 26, 1957, he accused his fellow board members of "crawling to Wright at the bidding of one of his vassals to bow and kiss his hand." One of the other board members, Walter Castro, shot back, "We didn't go to him like a bunch of sheep." Vera Schultz then reminded Fusselman that he chose not to go with the other board members when they went to interview Wright at his San Francisco office.[6]

Another objection Fusselman had was that he thought Wright's fee for the project was too high. Wright demanded 10 percent of the construction budget, at a time when most other American architects were charging 8 percent. In response, Marin County Planning Director Mary Summers pointed out that it was "quite inexpensive when you consider it includes the costs of a master plan for the site," which were usually paid for separately on large government projects. After discussing Fusselman's objections in detail, the board decided to move ahead with their initial choice. So on July 30, 1957, four of the board members signed a contract with Wright for him to be the architect of their new civic center. William Fusselman refused to sign the document.[7] He would soon launch a whole new line of attack against Wright, one that involved a bitter, vitriolic array of personal accusations, which nearly made Wright decide to withdraw from the project.

The day after the four board members had signed his contract, Wright made an appearance before a public meeting, attended by a large crowd at San Rafael High School, so he could explain his concept for the civic center to the community at large. Tiburon architect Henry Schubart introduced Wright, calling him "one of the greatest architects of all time." As he stepped up to the microphone, Wright responded with false modesty: "After all, it's not much to be the greatest architect in the world, because there aren't any great ones."[8]

Wright told the audience that they would be getting a "fresh, convenient, and beautiful civic center," with plenty of space for parking. The next day, the *Marin Independent Journal* ran an in-depth article on the meeting, reporting that Wright's "sharp wit and caustic observations kept the audience of about 600 applauding and laughing during a one-hour show," but that he parried all questions about what buildings would be included in his plans and what they would look like, as well as what the total cost of the project would be. He defined his philosophy of organic architecture as "building from the inside out and not from the outside in. Too many buildings are built from the four outer walls, and the inside made to fit." He also declared, "Civilization without a culture is like a man or woman without a soul. Culture consists of the love of beauty in the human spirit." Then he opened the question-and-answer session by saying, "Now you can tear me apart."[9]

One man asked how Wright would halt the "cancerous growth of present building developments that are ruining Marin County."

Wright replied, "Well—there's the atom bomb." Then he launched into a tirade about utility poles and wires, and tiny lots that were jamming homes side by side. "We've got to get out and abolish the realtor. I have hated him from the inception of my architectural career." Next he blamed the people themselves for their apathy by not demanding a higher quality in their developments. "If you are up for something better, you are going to get it," he declared. In referring to the ongoing controversy over his hiring for the civic center project, he asserted with typical arrogance that, "When people go for an architect, they should go on hands and knees as far as they can go to get the best, because the best isn't good enough." The meeting ended with Supervisor Castro telling the audience that Wright had signed a contract with the county the night before. Supervisor Fusselman was conspicuously absent from this event.[10]

Meanwhile, opposition to Wright had been voiced from other quarters. At the board of supervisors meeting on July 25, 1957, a Marin County Veterans Service officer named W. P. Duhamel objected vociferously to Wright's being chosen to design a veteran's memorial building as part of the civic center project. "We don't like his war record, and we don't want his name on our Veteran's Memorial Building." He went on to state, "We think Wright is a pacifist. From what I've heard, during World War II, Wright had several conscientious objectors among his men. His name was mentioned in the 1948 report of the Un-American Activities Committee, and I would say unfavorably." Duhamel concluded by saying, "It's all right if he designs it, I guess, as long as he keeps his name off of it." The supervisors ignored Duhamel's objections, and proceeded to pass a declaration restating their decision to draw up a contract with Wright.[11] Once again, Fusselman's was the lone dissenting vote. This incident proved to be the opening salvo in an ugly campaign to impugn Wright's patriotism and loyalty as an American citizen.

On August 2, 1957, the Marin County Board of Supervisors held a formal meeting intended to finalize its decision to proceed with Wright's plans for the civic center, and to inspect the site with him for the first time. Instead, it turned into a three-ring circus. A member of the American Legion from nearby Mill Valley named Bryson Reinhardt, who was a vocal anti-Communist, demanded the supervisors let him file a seven-page report accusing Wright of having "a record of active and extensive support of Communist views and enterprises." The meeting then erupted in acrimonious debate. The first one to speak was the architect himself. He labeled the charges "ridiculous" and "an unjustified insult that had been buried long ago. There's no substance in that. I'm a loyal American, and everybody knows it. Don't look at that, look at my record. I am what I am. If you don't like it, you can lump it. To hell with it all." Then he stood up and stalked toward the exit. Supervisor Castro tried to get him to turn around. "Do you mind—?" he

Marin County Supervisor Vera Schultz, c. 1974. Photograph by Emme Gilman. Courtesy of Emme Gilman Collection, Anne T. Kent California Room, Marin County Free Library.

Marin County Civic Center, early scale model with gold paint on roofs, and other structures never built, c. 1958. Courtesy of Harold Stockstad Slide Collection, Anne T. Kent California Room, Marin County Free Library.

asked. Wright responded angrily, "Yes, I do mind being insulted like this!" He continued to the exit doors then paused and turned around and waved his cane towards the audience. "This is an absolute and utter insult, and I will not be subject to it!" he thundered, before disappearing through the chamber doors.[12]

After Wright's exit, the supervisors had a heated discussion about whether they should allow Reinhardt's report to be read aloud and entered into the official record. Vera Schultz declared that Marin County had been "humiliated" by the introduction of this statement. She added, "This county does not look into the political beliefs of any of its employees. It is certainly most inappropriate that we should subject a man of Mr. Wright's caliber to the reading of such unfounded and unsubstantiated charges." Reinhardt objected to this, saying the charges weren't unfounded and could be documented. Then he admitted he "couldn't read Mr. Wright's mind" so he "did not know

if he is a card-carrying member of the Communist Party or not," but that this report contained only "certified and proven facts."

William Fusselman then moved that the report be read aloud before the entire board and entered into the official records. Vera Schultz informed him that both she and Supervisor Castro had already read it, and they did not feel it was worthy of being read to the entire board. Fusselman strenuously disagreed, saying the report had been prepared for the board by J. B. Matthews, a former staff member of the House Un-American Activities Committee who had worked as an investigator for Senator Joseph McCarthy.

Bryson Reinhardt praised Matthews, asserting that, "He's the outstanding authority on the Communist conspiracy."

Vera Schultz shot back, "Who says so?"

"Those who believe it is a deadly conspiracy and not just another political party," Reinhardt answered.[13]

The board adjourned without having the report read aloud. In the end it never *was* read before the board, since only Fusselman insisted on it. Some of the allegations in it included the charges that Wright had "expounded the Communist line on TV," praised Sovietism in a 1937 issue of *Soviet Russia Today,* wrote an article for the left-wing magazine *The Masses,* supported the Progressive Party's candidate Henry Wallace for president in 1948, was a sponsor of the Cultural and Scientific Conference for World Peace in 1949, and joined the American Committee for Protection of the Foreign Born. All of these activities were clearly a part of the Communist world conspiracy, the report concluded.[14]

As soon as the meeting adjourned, all the supervisors except Fusselman drove to the Santa Venetia hills to join Wright in inspecting the site for their future civic center. Wright was already walking briskly up and down the hillsides, despite his 90 years. When the supervisors caught up with Wright on one of the hilltops, he was talking to several reporters and local citizens. He gave the board a brief response to the charges that had been leveled at him during their meeting: "I do not believe there is a man in the United States who is more loyal to his nativity nor has done more for it than myself. Of course I'm an American—100 percent."

He went on to say a similar charge had been made against him about five years earlier while he was being considered for the design of the Air Force Academy in Colorado: "The American Legion said then it had a dossier on me, and said they would release it if the Defense Department hired me. I challenged them to bring out one single solid fact to show that I am disloyal. They haven't brought it out yet, and I thought the thing was dead." Wright cited one more example of false accusations against him. About 18 months before, when some Russian scientists were visiting the United States, a top Soviet architect had made a special visit to Wright. "I told him I loved his people as people and that I despised his government. The Russian people can come here anytime and be entertained by me. Is this communism? No, this is Americanism."[15]

Next, Wright shifted his focus to inspecting the 140-acre site. He walked all over the hilly terrain, ducking between the strands

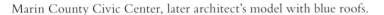

Marin County Civic Center, later architect's model with blue roofs.

of a barbed wire fence and climbing over another one. He jumped across several ditches and waded through knee-high grass and thistles, pausing every now and then to answer questions from the reporters and citizens, who were hard pressed to keep up with him. At the top of one of the hills, he stopped and declared, "Splendid. It's as beautiful as California can have." Then two 15-year-old Marin County girls asked Wright to pose for a photo with them. He readily agreed.

"Are you going to knock down these hills?" one of them asked.

"Not a single hill," the architect replied, smiling enthusiastically.

Another citizen asked him if he planned to make any further visits to the site before drawing up his formal set of plans.

"I don't have to drink a tub of dye to know what the color is," he replied.

Two hours after Wright had stormed out of the board meeting, he returned to the courthouse to sign a contract to design the new civic center. The contract called for a projected budget of $8,000,000, out of which Wright's office would receive a 10 percent fee for the master plan and design of the entire complex. Wright had to sign carbon copies of the contract, because County Clerk George Jones, Fusselman's ally, had failed to show up at a board meeting two days earlier with the contract for Wright to sign, and no copies of the contract were to be found in Jones's office. Vera Schultz said she was sure that this was a thinly veiled plot to prevent Wright from signing. But Supervisor Castro found a carbon copy in his pocket after they returned to the courthouse. So Frank Lloyd Wright finally was designated as the official architect of the Marin County Civic Center, although Fusselman would continue to try to thwart the construction of Wright's design over the next few years.[16]

Wright's concept for the civic center was quite simple, and at the same time a stroke of genius. As he had promised to the 15-year-old girls he spoke to when he inspected the site, his design called for leaving the hillsides intact. The main part of the complex was to be a low-lying, V-shaped set of two main wings (the Administration Building in the south wing and the Hall of Justice in the north wing), joined

Marin County Civic Center, Administration Building under construction looking north, c. 1961. Courtesy of Harold Stockstad Slide Collection, Anne T. Kent California Room, Marin County Free Library.

Portrait of Frank Lloyd Wright with quote from 1957 address to the citizens of Marin County. From 1962 dedication brochure for the Marin County Civic Center Administration Building. Courtesy of Anne T. Kent California Room, Marin County Free Library. Photograph by John Engstead.

"BEAUTY IS THE MOVING CAUSE OF NEARLY EVERY ISSUE WORTH THE CIVILIZATION WE HAVE, AND CIVILIZATION WITHOUT A CULTURE IS LIKE A MAN WITHOUT A SOUL. CULTURE CONSISTS OF THE EXPRESSION BY THE HUMAN SPIRIT OF THE LOVE OF BEAUTY.

"We will never have a culture of our own until we have an architecture of our own. An **architecture of our own** does not mean something that is ours by the way of our own **taste**. It is something that we have knowledge concerning. We will have it only when we know what constitutes a good building and when we know that the good building is not one that hurts the landscape, but is one that makes the landscape more beautiful than it was before that building was built. In Marin County you have one of the most beautiful landscapes I have seen, and I am proud to make the buildings of this County **characteristic** of the beauty of the County.

"Here is a crucial opportunity to open the eyes of not Marin County alone, but of the entire country to what officials gathering together might themselves do to broaden and beautify human lives."

FRANK LLOYD WRIGHT
From an address to the people of Marin County, July 1957

Front cover of 1962 dedication brochure for the Marin County Civic Center Administration Building. Courtesy of Anne T. Kent California Room, Marin County Free Library.

MARIN COUNTY CIVIC CENTER

in the middle by a shallow-domed library. These two wings branch out at about a 120-degree angle. The low-angled curves of the roofs on the two wings and the library dome reflect the shapes of the rounded hilltops on which this structure is perched, so that it almost appears to be a part of the landscape at first glance. Thus, one of Wright's largest and latest projects still conforms to his philosophy of "organic architecture." He further integrated this structure into the landscape by incorporating modified Spanish Colonial architectural features. The edges of the roofs are decorated with a repeating pattern of cutout, or perforated half circles, reflecting the arches one sees in the covered walkways surrounding the cloisters of old Spanish missions. Wright also chose a golden tan color for the walls of this structure, a hue that both blends in with the hillsides and is similar to the color of adobe brick on many old Spanish Colonial houses (he originally had chosen gold as the color for the roofs, but that was changed to a sky blue after his death by his widow,

Olgivanna, when it was determined the gold paint would quickly tarnish into a dirty brown).[17] The structural walls of both wings are made of concrete, while the roofs consist of concrete covered by a thick layer of polymer paint.

Both the 560-foot-long Administration Building and the 850-foot-long Hall of Justice have rows of arches on each level of their exteriors, creating arcades like those on Roman aqueducts in Spain or France.[18] An access road runs underneath the largest archway on the ground level of the four-story Administration Building, allowing entry to an ample parking area beyond, while two such archways span access roads under the four-story Hall of Justice. Once again, Wright kept a major promise to the citizens of Marin County: that his civic center would provide plenty of parking. One other distinctive feature of this main structure is the 172-foot-tall tower he placed near the juncture of the two wings. It overlooks a quiet patio, with a garden and a reflecting pool with a fountain. He intended this spire-shaped tower to transmit music, and made it adjacent to the domed Marin County Civic Center Library. These two features were important elements in Wright's concept of what the purpose of a local government complex should be: not just to dispense justice and mete out punishment to lawbreakers, but also to provide information and art, thereby contributing to the knowledge and

Marin County Civic Center, view of
Administration Building and Hall of Justice
(1957–69).

wisdom of its citizens (this spire was never actually used for transmitting as Wright had intended, but serves as a ventilation tower for the Administration Building).

The interior of the Administration Building is as distinctive and interesting as the exterior. Entering on the ground level beneath the wide archway, visitors pass through a set of bronze gates set in front of an escalator. These gates are embellished with an intricate pattern of vertical curls that resemble fountain spray motifs often found in Art Deco buildings of the 1930s. The escalator leads to the first of the three main levels of the building, which house the offices of various county departments and officials, as well as public restrooms and a cafeteria. The most striking feature of the building is the ceiling above the fourth level, which Wright designed in the form of a curved, clear glass skylight that bathes the open hallways below in natural light, and allows the people working below to look up at the open sky as they walk to and from various offices. The hallways have curved balconies along their outer edges, which provide views of the other hallways above and below them, and form a central light court with a powerful rhythm of repeated ellipses.

FACING: Marin County Civic Center, view of Administration Building looking east. ABOVE: Marin County Civic Center, entry gates to Administration Building.

At the eastern end of the Administration Building, on the top level, is the entrance to the Civic Center Library. The shallow-domed ceiling of the library is painted in a bright white color, and there are rounded light fixtures inserted into a gold-colored metal rim around the edges of the dome. A dome surrounded by "a ring of light" is reminiscent of the great rotunda of the Hagia Sophia in Istanbul, albeit on a much more modest scale. The library dome serves as a visual anchor for the two main wings of the civic center. The Hall of Justice veers off from this central point in a north-northwest direction. This four-story structure is integrated at its far end into a hillside, one of those hills Wright saw on his visit to the site and promised not to knock down. Buried partway into this hillside, and almost out of sight from below, is the county jail. Wright took the unusual step of placing the jail on the top level, so that prisoners could benefit from sunlight and fresh air during their incarceration. He explained this by saying,

ABOVE, LEFT: Marin County Civic Center, view of light well in Administration Building. ABOVE, RIGHT: Marin County Civic Center, detail of third and fourth levels of Administration Building. FACING: Marin County Civic Center, detail of second level of Administration Building from staircase.

"There is no use putting prisoners in the basement to preserve them. I put these devils condemned to eternal servitude on top where they could view nature."[19] (Wright was overlooking the fact that at that time county jails did not hold prisoners for more than one year in California.) The entire arcaded structure of the Hall of Justice is reflected in a man-made lagoon that runs along the eastern edge of the complex.

The civic center complex includes several other buildings that were part of Wright's original master plan. These include a U.S. Post Office, the only federal government building designed by Wright that was ever built. It is a round, low-lying, one-story building made of concrete, with a sweeping curved canopy above the entrance that has a flag-pole running through it, originally anchored by a globe. The post office is across the road from the Administration Building. Wright also designed the county fairgrounds across the lagoon, which include an exhibit pavilion, a children's island, and the Marin Veterans Memorial Auditorium.

A second public meeting was held on March 25, 1958 at the San Rafael High School auditorium, where over 700 Marinites had the opportunity to peruse a set of drawings of the civic center complex that had been produced by Wright's studio. The *Marin Independent Journal* ran a feature article the next day with a drawing of the Administration Building wing. An article in the *San Francisco Examiner* began with this subheading: "How to put $9 million worth of government center into Marin's sun burnt hills so you can hardly notice it, was illustrated in San Rafael last night by Frank Lloyd Wright."[20] At this meeting, Wright acknowledged that his estimated budget for the project had increased by $3 million from his preliminary estimates, but he claimed that the

FACING: Marin County Civic Center, courtyard with golden spire. ABOVE: Marin County Civic Center, view of library with domed ceiling.

Administration Building could be built for $2,750,000, or about $20 per square foot. Then he told reporters who were pestering him about the increased cost, "Simplicity is often expensive, you know; but in this case I think you will find it is economical."[21] All of the Marin County Board of Supervisors attended this public meeting, and stated their intention to give their unequivocal approval to Wright's plans—except for William Fusselman, who once again was conspicuously absent. As for the public response to Wright's plans, there were only a few negative comments, with one irate citizen asking, "How are we going to stop the county from spending our money on this monstrosity?" Fusselman quickly organized opposition to Wright's plans by reviving a dormant group: the Marin County Taxpayers Association. This group voted unanimously to oppose the project, then created a slide show detailing their objections, which was mounted in a bookmobile and driven all around the county to be shown to anyone who would listen. Yet despite such entrenched opposition, on April 28, 1958, the board of supervisors voted four to one to approve Wright's plans.[22]

Frank Lloyd Wright died on April 9, 1959, so the board voted a few days later to continue construction with the Frank Lloyd Wright Foundation. Wes Peters was named chief architect, and Aaron Green was appointed supervising architect. Construction on the Administration Building began on February 15, 1960, after bids were submitted and a contractor was chosen. Wright's widow, Olgivanna, was in attendance at the groundbreaking ceremony, and she gave her blessing to the entire project. Peters and Green were able to work from Wright's fairly detailed drawings to carry out his plan essentially as he had designed it.

Unfortunately, the organized opposition to Wright's plans was far from finished. On June 7, 1960, supervisors Vera Schultz and James Marshall lost their reelection bids, in part because of their support of the new civic center. The two new board members were opponents of the plan, so for the first time in five years the anti-Wright faction had a majority. But the new board didn't take office until January 1961, so an attempt to issue a stop order for a 90-day suspension of construction

ABOVE: Marin County Civic Center, third and fourth levels of Hall of Justice. FACING: Marin County Civic Center, Veterans' Memorial Auditorium.

and $250,000 escalators. A group of 46 taxpayers had written a letter to Governor Edmund G. Brown, protesting the way the board had approved this project and asking for an official investigation.[24] In the end, the swimming pool, an outdoor amphitheater, a restaurant, a senior citizens' center, and a children's zoo were never built, there was no investigation, and the final cost of the entire project, including the fairgrounds and the Veterans Memorial Auditorium, came to a grand total of $19,352,000.[25]

The stop order on the construction site was only in effect for one week. The work resumed on January 17, 1961, after the *Marin Independent Journal* polled its readers on whether to continue the project. The result was an overwhelming vote of support: 8,152 in favor, 1,225 against. Supervisor Fusselman and his group of naysayers finally had to admit defeat, as the board voted to rescind the stop order. In October 1961, the supervisors voted to change the color of the roof from gold to blue, in part to reflect the sky and the bay. The post office opened in May 1962, the first building to be completed. On October 13, 1962, the Administration Building was dedicated.[26]

was voted down by the lame-duck board's pro-Wright majority. On January 10, 1961, the new board voted three to two to halt construction and convert the site for use as a county hospital.[23] The opposition had been busy trying to rally grass roots efforts to halt the project even before Wright's death. In early March 1959, a lengthy article in the *San Francisco Examiner* described these efforts. It began, "A steadily growing number of Marin County taxpayers are denouncing the $13,800,000 county Civic Center project as 'a second Taj Mahal—a grandiose monument far beyond the needs and financial means of the taxpayers.'" The article went on to explain that Wright's original cost estimate had been inflated by what many citizens considered unnecessary expenditures, such as a swimming pool mounted on a hydraulic lift so it could also be used as a ballet stage, a huge artificial lagoon,

In November 1963, the board voted to commission the Frank Lloyd Wright Foundation to draw up a set of working drawings for the Hall of Justice. Green designed a series of circular courtrooms, which were not part of Wright's original plans. He also drew up the detailed plans for the jail within the overall concept that Wright had created. Other changes Green and Peters made mostly involved altering the sizes of certain rooms to suit the current needs of the county, and using movable walls in some offices to allow for easy adjustments of space usage in the future. Groundbreaking for the Hall of Justice occurred in 1966, and construction was completed in December 1969, under the supervision of Taliesin Associated Architects. The building opened to the public in January 1970.[27]

Since its completion, the Marin County Civic Center has been the setting for two feature films and a music video, as well as one tragic event that drew national media attention. August 7, 1970 is a date that many citizens of Marin County will remember for the rest of their lives. The Hall of Justice had just opened a few months earlier, and a high-profile criminal trial was being held in one of its courtrooms. James McClain, a San Quentin prisoner, was charged with assaulting a prison guard. He was representing himself before Judge Harold Haley, a 66-year-old native of San Rafael who had tried many cases involving violent felonies. McClain had called several San Quentin inmates to testify in his defense. One of them, Ruchell Magee, had just taken the witness stand when "all hell broke loose," as several witnesses described the incident later. Suddenly, Jonathan Jackson, a 17-year-old whose older brother George was awaiting trial for murdering a guard at Soledad State Prison, burst into the courtroom armed with a sawed-off shotgun, three

handguns, tape, and a wire under his overcoat. Jackson planned to seize Judge Haley as a hostage and hold him as a bargaining chip for his brother's freedom. He pulled out one of his handguns and ordered everyone to freeze. Then he tossed his other weapons to McClain, Magee, and a third convict, William Christmas, and ordered the guards to remove their shackles. The convicts taped the shotgun to the back of Haley's neck, then took Haley, Assistant District Attorney Gary Thomas, and three female jury members with them at gunpoint as they exited the building.

When the group got outside, they climbed into a getaway van. As the van drove under the south arch of the Hall of Justice, local law enforcement officers who had been gathering outside began firing their weapons at it. McClain, who was driving, was killed. Then one of the other convicts shot Judge Haley in the head, killing him instantly. Thomas grabbed one of the guns and shot Magee, Jackson, and Christmas, killing the latter two. A bullet fired by the officers pierced the van and hit Thomas, paralyzing him permanently below the waist. When the van came to a

stop and the shooting was over, the three women jurors were unharmed. Marin County later named the southern archway of the Hall of Justice for Judge Haley.[28]

George Lucas's first feature-length film, *THX 1138*, was partly filmed at the Marin County Civic Center. It starred Robert Duvall and Donald Pleasence, and was set in the future where the population is controlled by android policemen and mandatory drugs to suppress all emotions. The 1997 Hollywood feature film *Gattaca,* starring Ethan Hawke, Jude Law, and Uma Thurman, used the Marin County Civic Center as its main setting. This science fiction film also took place

ABOVE: Marin County Civic Center, U.S. Post Office (1957–62), the only federal building designed by Frank Lloyd Wright. RIGHT: Marin County Civic Center, view of Administration Building across lagoon.

in the future, when regular interplanetary trips by rocket were being made from a futuristic command center. The Administration Building was chosen as the site for this command center, and both its exterior and interior were used for many scenes, most of which were filmed at night when the county offices were closed. It was a fitting choice, since many observers over the years have described the complex as having a "space age" appearance, with the central spire resembling a rocket ship about to blast off. And in 2011, the music video *I Need a Doctor,* featuring hip-hop musicians Dr. Dre, Eminem, and Skylar Grey, was filmed inside the civic center.[29]

ABOVE: Marin County Civic Center, detail of loggias. BELOW: Marin County Civic Center, view of upper terrace of Administration Building. FACING: Marin County Civic Center, rooftops and spire of Administration Building.

Frank Lloyd Wright's unique vision for the Marin County Civic Center was perfectly suited to the rolling hillsides it graces. When the Administration Building opened in 1962, the *San Francisco Chronicle* ran an editorial with the heading "Marin Center Is a Thing of Beauty." It declared that, "Something of a miracle has been wrought in the Marin hills. Students of architecture and civic planning will doubtless use the Civic Center as a model for generations to come." The editors went on to state, "Already engineering groups have conducted studies of its structural elements, and lay visitors have been flocking to the building as they do to cathedrals in Europe."[30]

But it was Wright himself who best described the concept he was guided by in creating this masterpiece of public architecture. In comments he made to the public meeting he attended in San Rafael in July 1957, he summed up the goal he had in designing the civic center:

> *We will never have a culture of our own until we have an architecture of our own. . . . We will have it only when we know what constitutes a good building and when we know that the good building is not one that hurts the landscape, but is one that makes the landscape more beautiful than it was before the building was built. In Marin County you have one of the most beautiful landscapes I have seen, and I am proud to make the buildings of this county characteristic of the beauty of the county.*[31]

Anyone who has driven past the Marin County Civic Center on Highway 101 and looked closely at its elegant arcades as they connect the rounded hilltops they rest upon knows what a gift Frank Lloyd Wright gave to the people of Marin and the world. And anyone who doubts how much an integral part of the natural landscape Wright's complex has become needs only to engage in one very simple exercise—imagine Marin County without it.

CHAPTER 8

FROM COMMERCE TO RELIGION
Other Public Buildings in California

"Tell the people of the little church that I will help them out. . . . If I like the 'feel' of a job, I take it."
— Frank Lloyd Wright, to the building committee of Pilgrim Congregational Church, 1958

The Solomon R. Guggenheim Museum in New York City is one of Frank Lloyd Wright's most famous buildings. Indeed, it is one of the most recognized buildings in the world. It has been used as a setting or backdrop for dozens of TV shows and countless movies since it was completed in 1959. Yet a full decade earlier, Wright completed a small commercial building in San Francisco in which he pioneered the signature spiral interior ramp that is the most famous feature of the Guggenheim Museum. The V. C. Morris Gift Shop, at 140 Maiden Lane (just off Union Square), is an architectural gem that is reminiscent of its larger, younger cousin on the East Coast. Although Wright had completed his preliminary set of drawings for the Guggenheim in 1943, the V. C. Morris Gift Shop was the first building in which he actually used his innovative spiral ramp design.

Frank Lloyd Wright's first contact with Mr. and Mrs. Morris was in 1944, when they visited him at Taliesin West to ask him to design a residence for them. He produced a set of plans for a unique house that was in the form of a vertical three-story stacked cylinder, perched on a steep hillside 110 feet above the beach in the Sea Cliff section of San Francisco.[1] This radical design, different from anything else Wright had envisioned, was never built. However, the Morrises were intrigued enough with Wright's unorthodox thinking to ask him to design a gift shop, by remodeling an old warehouse they had bought along a narrow side street in the heart of San Francisco's retail district. The street was level,

thus avoiding the construction problems that their residential site created. Yet Wright's design for the gift shop was, in several ways, just as unconventional as his earlier proposal for their home.

The plans for the V. C. Morris Shop were completed in 1948, five years after Wright's preliminary drawings for the Guggenheim were drawn up. Thus there is no doubt that the Morris Shop served as a working prototype for the Guggenheim Museum; a trial run done on a much smaller scale. For the shop project, Wright incorporated both innovative features and design motifs he had used earlier in other buildings—often on the same part of the building. The best example of this is the unusual façade and entryway on Maiden Lane. Instead of having the front of the building sheathed in plate glass to display the wares for sale within and seduce passersby, he had the entire façade faced in narrow red brick. Around the entrance he placed a Romanesque-like set of concentric arches that emphasize the small, barrel-vaulted entry vestibule. Wright did this to create a sense of mystery and draw visitors to the front door to discover for themselves what lay within, thereby avoiding the "vulgar display of goods for sale" that was seen in traditional storefronts.[2] His use of a Romanesque archway around the main entrance was a motif he had used five decades earlier on the Francisco Terrace Apartments in Chicago (1895), and on some of his first Prairie houses in the Midwest, such as the Frank W. Thomas House in Oak Park, Illinois (1901), and the Francis and Mary Little House in Peoria, Illinois (1902).

Another innovative feature of the façade was Wright's placement of a row of lighted square acrylic plastic bricks in a horizontal

FACING: V. C. Morris Gift Shop, San Francisco (c. 1948–49), spiral ramp.

167

band that runs from the far right side of the building all the way along the waist-high platform that extends to the middle of the entryway. At night, these bricks gave off a soft yellow light from bulbs set into the wall behind them, and served as a subtle signpost to direct visitors to the front doorway. Wright's use of acrylic plastic for the exterior lights, as well as on the ceiling inside, was quite innovative, since this was a new material at that time.

After walking beneath the brick archway, visitors are ushered into the glass-and-metal-framed tunnel Wright designed to provide a transition from the noisy street into the quiet elegance of the gift shop's interior, with its array of fine and collectable merchandise that the Morrises were selling. Wright described this feature by telling Mr. and Mrs. Morris, "We are not going to dump your beautiful merchandise on the street but create an arch-tunnel of glass, into which a passerby may look and be enticed."[3]

Upon entering the Morris Shop, most visitors' attention is drawn upward along the dynamic angle of the curved ramp as it spirals towards the ceiling 40 feet above the floor. This ramp is made of white-painted reinforced concrete and lined with polished brass handrails, creating an elegant effect. Wright designed a drop-down ceiling to cover the entire width of the showrooms below. This

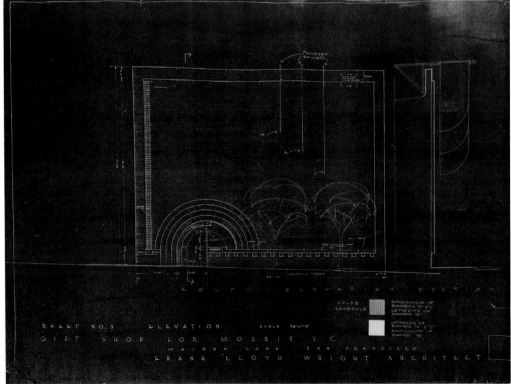

Top: V. C. Morris Gift Shop, exterior. Above: V. C. Morris Gift Shop, south elevation. Copyright © The Frank Lloyd Wright Foundation, Scottsdale, Arizona.

false ceiling consists of a repeating pattern of acrylic plastic panels that are molded into bubble shapes and set into square metal frames. These "bubble panels" admit sunlight for skylights above them, and their soft white surfaces seem to glow with an inner light. The overall effect of these unique features is to create the ambience of a bright, open, graceful space; one that invites visitors to linger and spend some time exploring all of the various treasures on display there.

Wright also designed all of the built-in display cases, cabinets, and tables that are arranged along the ground floor. These furnishings are all made with a walnut veneer. One of the largest cases, near the left rear corner of the shop as you enter, has a gilt ceiling above the glass-fronted display shelves. Wright also put built-in cabinets and counter-tops lining the curved walls behind the ramp. This provides an intriguing setting for some of the smaller sculptures for sale. These objects can be viewed through several port-hole windows Wright placed along the ramp. The use of these porthole windows is reminiscent of Art Deco commercial buildings of the 1930s, and was a feature Wright liked to use in many of his post-Deco-era public buildings, such as the Marin County Civic Center. The floors throughout the ground floor are made of beige-colored, polished concrete slabs.

V. C. Morris Gift Shop, detail of entry tunnel.

FACING: V. C. Morris Gift Shop, view of ramp and acrylic plastic ceiling. ABOVE: V. C. Morris Gift Shop, view of ground level with Frank Lloyd Wright–designed furniture.

The floor plan for the Morris Shop includes space for two corner offices. In the left front corner is a small room used for displaying antique Japanese prints, while the other small room in the right rear corner is used for the owner's office. Wright also designed a kitchen and two bathrooms on the ground floor. The total area of the shop is about 7,500 square feet, including a large basement for storing any overflow of merchandise that can't be kept in the display cases on the upper two levels. Construction of the shop took more than a year, and the supervising architects were Aaron Green and Walter Olds.[4] The Morrises opened the gift shop for business in 1949. They sold fine china and linens, as well as silver, gold, and crystal objects. They owned the shop until 1960, and there have been several owners since then. Over the past five decades, the shop has been used as a fine jewelry shop, a lady's dress shop, and a modern art gallery, among other things.[5]

In 1997, Raymond Handley bought the shop. He realized it needed a major restoration, so he hired Aaron Green out of retirement to supervise the renovation of the interior. This project took 11 months, and the new shop opened for business in December 1997. The City of San Francisco also required a total retrofit of the building for earthquake safety. So in 2002, Raymond's wife, Marsha, oversaw the completion of a seismic retrofit of the entire structure, which included stabilizing the brick façade on Maiden Lane. After this work was completed, the row of square, recessed lights along the façade became inaccessible from the inside, so the bulbs inside them could no longer be changed. Other than this detail, the building has retained nearly all of its original Wright-designed features. The shop is now known as the Xanadu Gallery, and specializes in antique Asian works of art, as well as featuring Oceanic, pre-Columbian, and African sculptures, and other objects.

Marsha Handley sees a historic continuity in the type of shop she runs in this unique building and the original shop Wright designed in 1948. "Having worked in this very special space and displaying our art here for many years, it seems to me that our

V. C. Morris Gift Shop, ground-floor display cases with gold ceiling.

ABOVE: V. C. Morris Gift Shop, view of ground-floor display cabinets. BELOW: V. C. Morris Gift Shop, detail of ceiling.

collection of Asian antiquities blends in quite well with Wright's design. Since Mr. Wright was a collector of antique Asian art himself, especially old Japanese prints, his design meshes beautifully with the objects we have on display now."[6] The V. C. Morris Gift Shop became an official San Francisco Landmark in 1975.

▼ ▼ ▼ ▼ ▼

Although religious structures did not constitute a major portion of Frank Lloyd Wright's total output, he did design eight such buildings during his career. The variety of Wright's religious buildings covers quite a wide range, including an Arts and Crafts Unitarian chapel in Spring Green, Wisconsin, in 1886, his first completed commission; Unity Temple in Oak Park, Illinois, a synthesis of Prairie and Arts and Crafts styles, designed in 1905 and completed in 1908; two modernistic chapels on the campus of Florida Southern College, built between 1938 and 1954; the futuristic Beth Sholom Synagogue in Elkins Park, Pennsylvania, designed in 1954; and the round, Space Age–looking Annunciation Greek

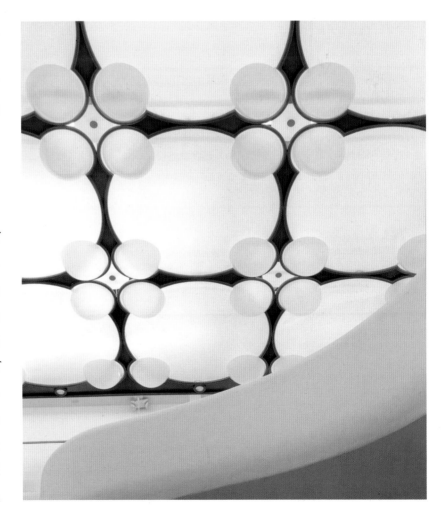

Orthodox Church in Wauwatosa, Wisconsin, designed in 1956.

The last religious building Frank Lloyd Wright designed, and one of the most unorthodox of all his commissions, was the Pilgrim Congregational Church in Redding, California. Designed in 1958 and not completed until 1961, it remains one of Wright's least-known buildings, and is the only Wright-designed religious structure ever built on the West Coast. Pilgrim Congregational Church sits above the banks of Jenny Creek, at 2850 Foothill Boulevard, about three miles west of Interstate 5. Redding is an old mining and lumber town of over 90,000 residents two hours south of the Oregon border.[7] Besides its Wright-designed church, the town boasts the famous Sundial Bridge, designed by the internationally acclaimed Spanish architect Santiago Calatrava, as well as homes designed by famed California architects Bernard Maybeck and Julia Morgan.

Wright's commission for Pilgrim Congregational Church had its origins in 1957, when Reverend Ray Welles joined a building committee seeking to find an architect for his growing congregation's future church. In 1956, a 4.6-acre site was chosen along the creek to build the church. In 1958, Reverend Welles announced that Frank Lloyd Wright had agreed to design their new building. A member of the building committee had placed a call to Taliesin West, requesting Wright design their church after they had rejected eight other architects. The request was relayed to Wright in New York City, where he was working on the Guggenheim Museum. Wright told the Taliesin staff to give this reply: "Tell the people of the little church that I will help them out. . . . If I like the 'feel' of a job, I take it."[8]

While the committee had been interviewing other architects, students from Shasta College had surveyed the lot and produced detailed site drawings. When these drawings were sent to Wright to study, he remarked that he'd never seen a better job of terrain drawings. Working from these drawings, Wright produced a plan for an A-frame-type complex with four intersecting wings, anchored by a tall stone tower topped with a metal spire. The roofs of these wings would be hung from a series of redwood bents, resembling a whale's skeleton. The style of this building was dubbed "pole and boulder Gothic" in a notation by Wright himself on his preliminary drawings.[9]

In March 1958, the building committee had sent Wright a document called "What Our Building Must Express." It included this vision: "We believe that creative architecture will make people aware of the resources of our Christian faith. Men thirst for God and are particularly desperate in our time. For many people, God is transcendent and distant. Our building ought then to reflect the intimacy and eminence of God as well as his majesty." Though Wright did not come in person to see the site, the committee members met with Wright in his office in San Francisco, after the drawings for the Marin County Civic Center were published in the local press. As the members sat in a tight circle around Wright discussing their project with him, he reached over and tapped Reverend Welles's knee and said to him, "Well, Domini [a familiar Scottish term for a reverend], how long do you suppose we'll keep building churches?" A lively discussion ensued about the place of religion in modern American society and Wright's own strong religious faith, from which he'd never wavered throughout his life.[10]

During the committee's visit, Wright explained that his concept for their church represented a tent form, which symbolized the ancient dwellings of Israel. He told them the church would appear to grow out of the ground, since it would nestle comfortably into its hillside setting, and the fitted stone walls and wooden poles supporting the roof

FACING: Pilgrim Congregational Church, Redding, California (1958–61), east façade. ABOVE: Pilgrim Congregational Church, view of west façade. BELOW: Pilgrim Congregational Church, detail of rubblestone wall.

ABOVE: Pilgrim Congregational Church, view of sanctuary. FACING: Pilgrim Congregational Church, view of stage and pulpit.

would blend in well with the stony, wooded landscape. The pulpit area in the sanctuary would resemble a cave, and worshipers would walk down a set of steps into the sanctuary to suggest a return to God's creation. Then Wright summed up by telling them, "your faith has emotion in it, and so does your building."[11]

The original plans called for a fellowship hall and adjoining offices to be built on a north–south axis, with an adjacent education wing running diagonally southeast off the central section. At the north end was to be a large sanctuary that would run diagonally northwest off the central section and a small chapel running diagonally northeast off the sanctuary. The floor plan was based on a series of intersecting equilateral triangles, a system Wright often used in his later public buildings. The final set of drawings was dated April 1959, the month Wright died.

Construction began in the summer of 1960, after some difficulty in finding a local contractor who could carry out Wright's unusual plans. The work was done under the supervision of John Rattenbury, Tony Puttnam, and Aaron Green of Taliesin Associated Architects. In the end, only the fellowship hall, education wing, and offices were built. Construction of these sections was completed in late December 1961, just in time for the congregation to celebrate Christmas mass in the fellowship hall. The church has used this space as their sanctuary ever since. Both the education wing and the office section have been remodeled in recent years, and a basement was added to provide more classroom space. The bents, or poles, were changed from redwood to concrete, due to cost considerations, as well as the limited structural strength of redwood. Wright had chosen redwood because he mistakenly assumed Redding was surrounded by redwood forests.[12]

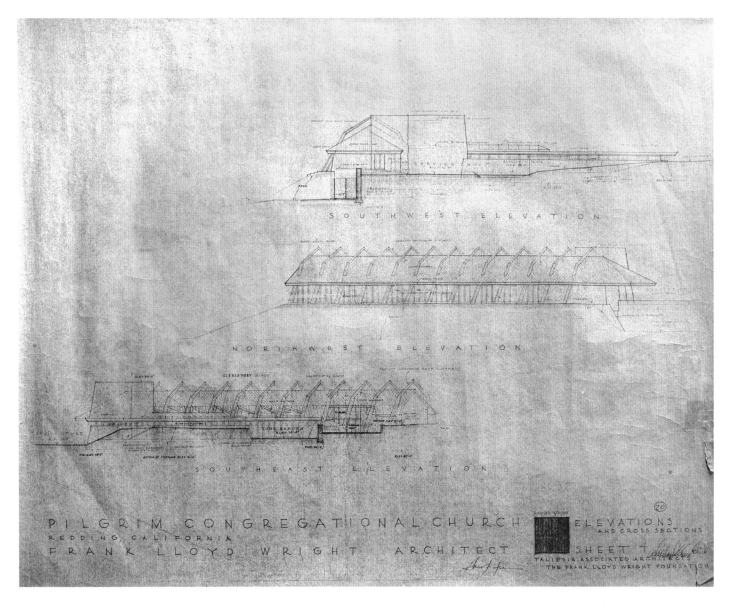

Pilgrim Congregational Church, blueprint of southwest, northeast, and southeast elevations. Copyright © The Frank Lloyd Wright Foundation, Scottsdale, Arizona.

The main entrance to the Pilgrim Congregational Church is on the eastern side, down a set of polished concrete steps. These steps, as well as the concrete floor and steps throughout the sanctuary, are stained Wright's favorite Cherokee red color. The first feature one notices in the sanctuary is a steeply pitched ceiling, which rises to a point in the middle and is lined with massive beams. These beams were originally made of Douglas fir, but were replaced with cedar planks after a fire in 1992 required some restoration of the ceiling. The wood window frames were also replaced with metal framing at that time. The most interesting part of the sanctuary is the front, where a short set of steps rises up to a stage and the pulpit. Wright designed a large wooden cross for the stage, anchored to the wall behind the pulpit.

The walls of the sanctuary are made out of a variety of local rocks set into concrete. These rocks vary greatly in color, size, and shape, and they create a rich set of textures and visual patterns. Wright used this same technique for the walls surrounding the sunken garden terrace, adjacent to the education wing. All of these fieldstones were gathered by members of the congregation and brought to the site during construction. At the south end of the sanctuary there is a massive two-story stone tower, made out of the same materials. A door set in the rear left corner of the stage leads into a small kitchen on the ground floor. The second floor was originally used as the pastor's office, but is now used as a storage area.

The head of the Pilgrim Congregational Church at the time of this writing, Reverend Ann Corrin, described those qualities she liked best about the building: "Anyone who has a creative spark, when they walk into the church it feeds that in them. I've noticed that this building has a creative spirit, one that inspires artists and musicians. We frequently have musical events here, and all of the musicians say they love playing here, and that the acoustics are really perfect."[13]

▼ ▼ ▼ ▼ ▼

During his 66 years of independent practice, Frank Lloyd Wright designed dozens of commercial buildings. Besides retail shops, he also designed corporate headquarters, banks, a gas station, a restaurant, law offices, and even a real estate office, despite his stated disdain for that profession (see Chapter 7). Wright also designed four medical clinics late in his career, including the Meyers Medical Clinic in Dayton, Ohio (1956); the Fasbender Medical Clinic in Hastings, Minnesota (1957); and the Lockridge Medical Clinic in Whitefish, Montana (1958). But the first medical clinic he designed was the Kundert Medical Clinic in 1954 in San Luis Obispo, California.

This is also the most intimate of his medical clinics in scale, and many historians feel it's the most charming in ambience.

San Luis Obispo is a quaint old California town of about 45,000 people on the central coast. It lies just 30 miles south of famed Hearst Castle, built by William Randolph Hearst and designed by America's first independent woman architect, Julia Morgan. Most of the nearly one million tourists who visit Hearst Castle each year never venture into the historic town of San Luis Obispo and have no idea it has an intact architectural gem by Frank Lloyd Wright.

The Kundert Medical Clinic (now called the Tway Clinic) sits at 1106 Pacific Street, at the northeast corner of Pacific and Santa Rosa streets near the historic central business district. Dr. Karl Kundert was an ophthalmologist with a thriving practice when he first wrote to Frank Lloyd Wright in 1950 about designing a new clinic for him. He was familiar with Wright's buildings from

Kundert Medical Clinic, San Luis Obispo, California (1954–56), southwest façade.

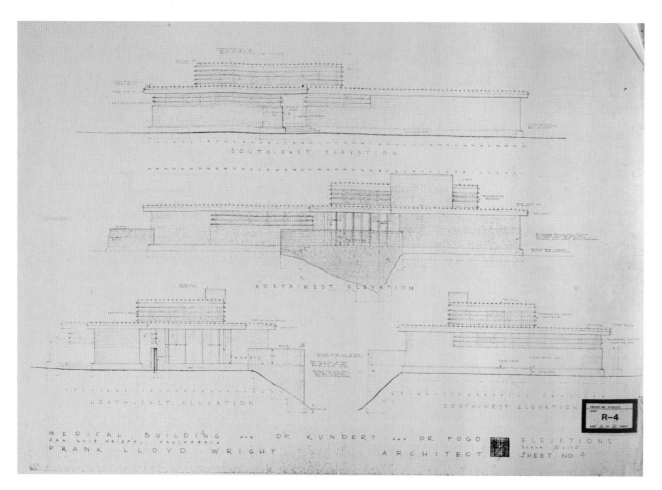

LEFT: Kundert Medical Clinic, blueprint of southeast, southwest, northeast, and northwest elevations. Copyright © The Frank Lloyd Wright Foundation, Scottsdale, Arizona. BELOW: Kundert Medical Clinic, view of northwest façade.

having seen many of them while growing up in Wisconsin.[14] He sent Wright flowchart studies of his patient load, as well as photos and a map of his lot. The site he chose, a narrow, uneven, irregular corner lot that sits just above San Luis Creek, with a steep ravine along its northern edge, presented more than a minor challenge. Wright's solution was to orient the building primarily on an east–west axis, with the front entrance on Santa Rosa Street. The low, horizontal massing, the flat roofline along the two street sides, and the undisturbed woodsy ravine along the north side, give the 2,500-square-foot building the appearance of nestling comfortably into its lush creekside setting. Wright used warm red brick for the façade of the clinic, and placed a triple clerestory with a repeating geometric pattern along the upper walls of the waiting room and to the right of the front entrance.

Wright's original plan called for concrete block construction, but local building codes required him to switch to brick, which is more in keeping with the façades of other commercial buildings in the area. Wright completed

Kundert Medical Clinic, view of entryway and reception area.

a set of plans in 1954, but Dr. Kundert requested that the two outside walls be moved two feet out to provide more room for his staff to treat their patients. The final plans were drawn up in 1955, and the construction took five months. The building was completed in 1956, under the supervision of Aaron Green. Wright was busy working on dozens of other projects around the country during that time, but he did visit the site two times: once briefly just before construction began, and once when it was nearly finished.[15]

Before construction could begin on the building itself, a massive, wedge-shaped slab of concrete had to be poured to create a retaining wall for the hillside and stabilize the foundation. This was accomplished without altering the course of San Luis Creek. The floor plan of the clinic is basically a large "L" shape, with the short side running along Pacific Street and the long side running up Santa Rosa Street. Both of these wings have a windowless room at the end, originally designed for eye exams and treatments. Wright used a grid pattern with two-foot squares for this structure, and the overall style is Usonian, adapted for commercial use. There is a concrete patio with a three-foot-tall wall around it, which provides a pleasant view of the creek for staff during breaks. Wright placed a parking pad, with space for eight cars, at the rear of the lot. He had the roof covered in tar and gravel. Surprisingly, this was one of Wright's few flat roofs that didn't leak profusely shortly after it was finished. However, there was some leakage near the chimney due to loose bricks in that section of the roof, which allowed rain to seep in through the mortar. Dr. Kundert soon had this problem fixed, and the roof stopped leaking.[16]

The main entrance to the clinic is down a wide cement slab path leading from the sidewalk. The cement is scored in square panels and painted classic Cherokee red, which is the same material Wright used for the floors throughout the clinic. This pathway, and the red brick walls flanking the wide glass-paneled front door, give visitors a feeling of being invited into a welcoming space. Upon entering, the first thing one notices is the spacious central waiting room, with its soaring, 14-foot-high ceiling paneled in mahogany. The ceiling is hipped at the corners, and lined with horizontal wood panels that emphasize its height. Just below these panels Wright placed a triple clerestory made of milk glass, with its intriguing cutout wooden decorative patterns. The north and east walls of this room are made from solid walls of banded glass doors, set into six-and-a-half-foot-tall wooden frames. These doors have piano hinges that allow them to be opened outwards onto the patio, to bring the outdoors indoors on mild days. There is a massive, brick-faced, open-hearth fireplace with a ceiling-high flue in the southwest corner of the room, and built-in wooden seating along the south side. The receptionist's desk is in the southeast corner, and sits behind a row of wood shelving below eye level, which gives some privacy to the receptionist while still allowing full eye contact with the patients. These shelves are decorated with the same cutout geometric pattern that lines

Kundert Medical Clinic, view of waiting room.

the clerestory. These features create a warm, peaceful ambience for the patients, one that makes the experience of sitting in a waiting room of a doctor's office much more pleasant than it usually is.

The rest of the interior is divided into 11 individual exam rooms, a few small offices, and three bathrooms, as well as a break room for the staff. Most of the exam rooms are arranged along the long wing facing Santa Rosa Street. In a remodel of the building done in 1992, the walls of some of the exam rooms were moved out further into the hallways to make more space for the doctors who used them.

Dr. Kundert operated his ophthalmology clinic here until he retired in 1986, and after that the building sat empty for six years. Then Dr. Kenneth Tway opened a cardiovascular clinic in the facility, after he remodeled some of the exam rooms. This clinic still occupies the site as of this writing. The building has maintained its structural integrity quite well over the past six decades or so since it was finished. During the heavy rains in the winter of 1967–68, San Luis Creek rose to 50 feet, well above its flood stage. The building might have been severely damaged, but because of the massive concrete retaining wall and the heavy, reinforced concrete slab Wright placed under the foundation for seismic stability, the clinic weathered the flood without any structural damage.[17]

▼ ▼ ▼ ▼ ▼

The heart of the Beverly Hills shopping district on Rodeo Drive, with its kitschy, often garish imitations of Greek and Roman temples attached to trendy storefronts, is hardly the place one would expect to find a futuristic Frank Lloyd Wright–designed courtyard of small, inconspicuous shops. But right in the center of this world-famous retail district, at 332 North Rodeo Drive, Wright designed the Anderton Court Shops in 1952. Thousands of tourists walk past these shops every day without realizing their architectural significance. Indeed, this structure bears little resemblance to any of Wright's other commercial buildings, let alone any of the buildings around it.

Between 1907 and 1952, Frank Lloyd Wright designed a total of seven stores in Illinois and California, including two art galleries.

The Anderton Court Shops, built for local businesswoman Nina Anderton, is the only Wright-designed shopping center, large or small, that was ever built on the West Coast. It is also the last building Wright completed in the Los Angeles area. These shops, wedged into a narrow lot on Rodeo Drive, were placed on the National Register of Historic Places in 2004.[18]

At first glance from across the street, the Anderton Court Shops have an almost *Wizard of Oz*/Emerald City appearance, or perhaps that of a scaled-down Mormon temple. The dominant feature is a tall, pointed concrete spire that rises about 15 feet above the middle of the structure. This spire has serrated edges that tilt upward, much like Buddhist temple finials. This motif was used on some earlier Art Deco–era buildings in California, and the shape of this spire is vaguely reminiscent of the much larger one Wright designed for the Marin County Civic Center several years later.

BELOW: Anderton Court Shops, Beverly Hills, California (1952), Art Deco concrete spire. FACING: Anderton Court Shops, view from Rodeo Drive.

The overall shape of the building forms a shallow "V," which opens toward the sidewalk. Wright designed four small shops on the first two levels, around a central, angled ramp. This ramp tilts upward at a gentle angle, and allows access to each of the shops. On the third level, Wright designed a penthouse apartment. In recent years, the retail space here has been divided into six smaller shops. The façade of the building is marked by long concrete balconies on the second and third levels, which line the edges of the ramp and run all the way across the front of the third story along the north side. The floors of the ramp have a scored, diamond-shaped pattern, similar to Wright's Usonian houses. Wright originally planned for the shop windows to be set back from the edges of the ramp, but since then, eight-foot-tall display windows have been installed out to the sidewalk at the north end of the first and second stories. Other changes that have been made to Wright's original design include attaching business signs to the balconies, and painting the stucco exterior white with black trim, instead of the original buff color offset by oxidized copper on the trim and the spire.[19]

Nevertheless, the Anderton Court Shops retain their Late Modern, Space Age character. Perhaps the best way to appreciate Wright's aesthetic concept for this building is to walk up the ramp to the third level and look down the narrow, open courtyard that runs to the back wall. Wright had two large porthole window motifs embossed into the wall at eye level on the right side. A squat, square tower rises above the wall at the back of the courtyard, a part of the original penthouse. When the afternoon sun forms strong diagonal shadows across this courtyard, it creates a Cubist-like effect, resembling an early abstract composition by Picasso or Georgia O'Keeffe.

ABOVE: Anderton Court Shops, side view of shop fronts. FACING: Anderton Court Shops, upper level of courtyard from central staircase.

CHAPTER 9

NORTH BY NORTHWEST

Houses in Oregon and Washington

"Well—it's an illegitimate child—but like all illegitimate children, it's the most beautiful."
— Frank Lloyd Wright about the Griggs House, c. 1949

The Pacific Northwest is one of the most breathtaking regions within the lower 48 states. Almost every part of Washington and Oregon is close to the natural beauty that is the defining feature of this section of the country. Even the major urban centers of Portland, Tacoma, and Seattle are surrounded by some of the most impressive works of nature in the United States: magnificent Mount Hood with its year-round snowpack, visible from all around the greater Portland area; the wide, deep, blue waters of Puget Sound flowing past Tacoma and Seattle; and the rugged grey peaks and lush evergreen forests of the Olympic Peninsula, which dominate the horizon from nearly everywhere in northwestern Washington.

It surprises even many Frank Lloyd Wright fans to know that he designed four houses in Washington and Oregon in the 1950s, near the end of his career. Of these four homes, all have retained nearly every feature Wright designed for them. His three houses in Washington are still in their original settings, while the one in Oregon was moved from a farm about 25 miles farther north, and is now operated as a historical museum open to the public. The sites of the three houses in Washington are, in a word, magnificent; they all have lovely views of the natural beauty that inspired Wright to design them. And they are still occupied as private residences, with most of their Wright-designed furniture and built-ins still in use.

The Conrad and Evelyn Gordon House was originally designed in 1956 for a site near Wilsonville, Oregon, a small community

on the southern outskirts of Portland. This site was along a bend in the Willamette River, at the edge of 550 acres of open farmland the Gordons had owned since 1940. Conrad Gordon was a soap salesman, and Evelyn worked as a secretary for her father's commercial laundry business. They began writing to Frank Lloyd Wright in the mid-1940s about designing a new home for them on their farmland. At that time they had two young sons and a daughter living at home. They received no reply from Wright to their first few letters, so in March 1956 they decided to go to Taliesin West to try to meet with him in person.

An apprentice they met at Taliesin decided to help them by arranging an appointment with Mr. Wright. He interviewed them extensively, asking them about the site and their lifestyle. They told him the waterfront portion of their farm had views of the river in two directions and a magnificent view of Mount Hood, and pointed out the rolling farmland and deciduous trees all around, such as alders and maples (they later sent Wright a site survey and photos of their farm). Evelyn also mentioned that she played a baby grand piano, a fact that appealed to the music-loving Wright, who was an amateur musician himself. Intrigued by the features of their site and the idea of designing a residence in one of the few states he had never built in before, Wright agreed to design their new residence. After working on the design off and on for several months, he mailed them a complete set of preliminary drawings on December 29, 1956. Wright had designated a former apprentice who lived in Oregon, Burton Goodrich, to be the supervising architect.[1]

FACING: Brandes House, Sammamish, Washington (1952–53), west façade.

Gordon House, Silverton, Oregon (1956–64), north end.

Gordon House, west façade.

After studying Wright's plans, the Gordons telephoned him on January 14, 1957 to discuss the details. After their conversation they sent Wright a letter in which they expressed their pleasure at the thought of having him design their home: "We enjoyed our visit with you today, and we are both overjoyed that you are going to design our house. The preliminary sketches are acceptable to us, and we hope that you can finish the working drawings in time for us to get started with construction by March 15, 1957. We are inclosing our check for 5% of the original estimated cost, and believe that with Mr. Goodrich's supervision and service, we can keep within the $25,000 limit."[2]

Alas, such was not to be the case. When the Gordons got the final set of plans later that year, they put them out to bid and were surprised to discover that no Oregon contractor would give a bid that was anywhere near their budget limit of $25,000. In fact, the bids ranged from $56,000 to $125,000! So they had to put off constructing the house for a few years, until they could save the funds needed. In 1962, they sold their farm, keeping a 22-acre site along the waterfront for their new home. They began construction in early 1963, and in April 1964 finally moved in. The final cost of building their dream home came to $56,000.[3]

The Gordon House is now located at the edge of the Oregon Garden at 869 West Main Street in the charming Victorian town of Silverton, Oregon. Its current site is in the middle of a grassy knoll, bordered by tall oak trees (the house was oriented at its new site in the same direction it originally faced at its original location). When visitors approach the front entrance, on the south side of the one-and-a-half-story house, the first thing they notice is the sweeping horizontal massing of the home, with its large wooden balconies extending several feet from the east and west ends. The flat roof is punctuated by two low, square concrete pads: one is the top of the chimney for the living room fireplace, and the other is a ventilation shaft for the kitchen. The exterior walls of the second-story bedrooms at the south end are sheathed in clapboards made of western red cedar. The rest of the exterior walls are covered in pink rose–colored concrete blocks. Floor-to-ceiling windows line the east and west walls of the living room/dining room wing of the house, which extends north off the entry wing. Wide

Gordon House, east side.

overhanging eaves in the form of trellises shelter the living room wing, providing shade for the Cherokee red concrete slab terraces lining this section of the house. Along the southwest and north walls of the living room wing, Wright placed multiple rows of wood fretwork in geometric patterns, which is the most distinctive feature of the Gordon House (a drawing of this decorative fretwork is used as the logo of the Gordon House Conservancy).

The style of the Gordon House is clearly Usonian, as are the three other residences Wright designed in the Pacific Northwest. The floor plan of this 2,133-square-foot house is T-shaped, with the head of the "T" at the south end. Wright's design was based on a set of plans *Life* magazine had published in 1938, under the heading "Frank Lloyd Wright Plans a 'Little Private Club.'" These plans were for a T-shaped, one-and-a-half-story residence with a flat roof, made of concrete blocks and wood siding.[4] This was an early public airing of Wright's Usonian House concept, which he used almost verbatim for the Bernard Schwartz House in Two Rivers, Wisconsin (1939). For the Gordons, Wright essentially created a simplified version of the plan he had published in *Life*,

with specific modifications to fit the lifestyle of his clients. Some of the modifications were expanding the carport that runs off the southeast corner of the house to three bays, decreasing the size of the basement to reduce construction costs, and adding a small alcove at the top of the stairs to accommodate Evelyn's spinning loom.

The main entrance is through a set of picture glass double doors, beneath an overhang. These double doors lead into a narrow entry hall, with the kitchen and a small office to the left. The kitchen retains all the original built-in appliances, over-the-counter lighting, and red Formica countertops. There is a light well/ventilation shaft above the stove, with a skylight at the top. Wright placed a small dining area adjacent to the kitchen, which is in the southwest corner of the living room wing. The spacious living room has an unusually high ceiling for a Usonian house. This impressive room is 35 feet long by 20 feet wide, with a 12-foot-tall ceiling. At the north end is a comfortable library alcove, with built-in seating along the wall. Above these seats are four rows of fretwork friezes, while the top of the dining alcove has five rows of the same design. There is a fireplace set into the east wall, with con-

LEFT: Gordon House, living room. ABOVE: Evelyn Gordon, 1966. Courtesy of Gordon Family Collection, Gordon House.

crete block facing. The tall picture windows that line the walls here allow lovely views of the surrounding trees, as well as Mount Hood in the distance to the east, and the Willamette Valley to the west. The floors in this room, as in all of the rooms, are made of concrete slabs stained Cherokee red, and scored with a seven-foot-square pattern, the largest geometric pattern Wright used for the floor plan of any of his Usonian houses. There is a radiant heating system in the house, with hot water pipes placed on a gravel bed beneath the concrete floor.

In the southeast corner of the first floor is the master suite, with an extra three-quarter bath. This room is darker than the rest of the house due to its having smaller windows, at Evelyn's request. There is also a laundry room

Gordon House, library alcove.

Gordon House, detail of living room.

in this section. A cedar staircase to the left of the entry hall leads to two more bedrooms upstairs. These bedrooms are connected by a gallery that runs along the south wall. The gallery has two rows of the same fretwork friezes as in the living room along the top of the walls, and cedar storage cabinets line the lower walls. There is a full bath between these bedrooms, which is more spacious than most Usonian bathrooms. Both of the upstairs bedrooms have built-in cabinets, and each has its own deep balcony. The bedroom on the east side of the second floor is the larger one, and it has banded, floor-to-ceiling picture glass windows, which double as doors that open onto the balcony. There is a built-in

desk here, and built-in bookshelves line the walls. The ceilings in both bedrooms, as well as in the living room wing, are paneled in cedar-faced plywood.

Evelyn Gordon lived happily in her custom-designed home for 33 years, until her death in 1997 (Conrad died in 1979). After her death, her middle child, Ed, became executor of the estate, and put the property on the market with an initial asking price of $3.3 million. There were no offers at that price, and the house finally sold in September 2000 for $1.1 million to David and Carey Smith. They asked for the house to be removed from the list of Clackamas County Historic Landmarks so they could get a demolition permit

ABOVE: Gordon House, east end bedroom. RIGHT: Gordon
House, kitchen.

and build a new house on the property. This alarmed local preservationists, who asked the Frank Lloyd Wright Building Conservancy to organize a nationwide effort to save the Gordon House. The FLWBC is a nonprofit group based in Chicago that is dedicated to preserving Frank Lloyd Wright's built legacy. After a protracted legal battle that lasted several months, the Smiths finally agreed to give the house to the FLWBC on the stipulation that it be moved to another property within 105 days at the group's expense, and the Smiths would receive a large tax deduction for this donation.[5]

The FLWBC received three proposals for new sites for the Gordon House. They accepted the one from the Oregon Garden, which then created a partnership with the City of Silverton to obtain legal title to the house and move it to the edge of their 80-acre garden tract, with its own one-acre easement. The house had to be disassembled into several sections before the move, using the original set of working plans. Then starting in February 2001, these sections were loaded onto flatbed trucks and driven 25 miles to the new site. The final section arrived at the Oregon Garden

in April 2001, and the work of reassembling the house began. When this was completed, the house was opened to the public as a museum in the summer of 2001. Since then, well over 100,000 people have visited the house. The Gordon House was added to the National Register of Historic Places in 2004.[6]

Washington State is known for its lush, green landscapes and fresh, clear lakes and streams. On the outskirts of Tacoma, near the banks of Chambers Creek, Frank Lloyd Wright designed his first of three houses in Washington in 1946, for Chauncey and Johanna Griggs. They had purchased a 10-acre lot in what is now the community of Lakewood in 1939. The site is near the foot of a rolling hill, and has several acres of open grassland bordered by evergreens and various deciduous trees including birch, alder, and Japanese maple. Chauncey Griggs interviewed six architects after they had decided to build a spacious home in the middle of this property. They needed room for

BELOW: Griggs House, Lakewood, Washington (1946–54), view from Chambers Creek. FACING, TOP: Griggs House, view of east side. FACING, BOTTOM: Frank Lloyd Wright drawing of Griggs House, c. 1946. Copyright © The Frank Lloyd Wright Foundation, Scottsdale, Arizona.

FOR MR AND MRS C. L. GRIGGS   FRANK LLOYD WRIGHT ARCHITECT

their three children, as well as an area for entertaining during social events. Chauncey was in the lumber business, importing and exporting logs to and from Japan after World War II. His company had installed ski lifts before the war on nearby Mount Rainier and two other sites. Wright was the last architect Chauncey contacted, after rejecting all the others. He flew to Taliesin West in 1945 to meet with Wright. When Griggs told Wright that he interviewed five other architects, including William Wurster, Wright replied, "Well, I see you went from bad to Wurster." Wright then agreed to draw up a set of preliminary drawings for Mr. and Mrs. Griggs, which he

sent them in 1946. The Griggses subsequently chose a local architect, Allen Liddle, to create the final set of working drawings. According to Mark Griggs, Chauncey's only son, after the house was completed some years later, one of Wright's staff showed Mr. Wright a photo of it, and noticing the modest changes Liddle had made in his original design, Wright commented, "Well—it's an illegitimate child—but like all illegitimate children, it's the most beautiful."[7]

Construction on the Griggs House did not begin until the late 1940s, but was plagued by unexpected delays and was not completed until October 1954. These delays were caused by the rapid rise in construction costs and building materials after World War II. Wright's plans originally called for the walls of the house to be built of stone, but in order to cut expenses, Wright agreed to change this to solid concrete blocks. Wright's design envisioned a large single-story home, with a soaring shed-style roof that is cantilevered 14 feet out over a wide, 1,200-square-foot terrace on the east side. This sheltered terrace is made out of local black river rock set into concrete. The roof is tilted sharply upward at a very steep angle over the southeast corner of the house. Wright's plans originally called for the roof to reach a plateau on this end, but recent leakage problems from the heavy Northwest rains caused Mark Griggs to redesign this section to include the steep pitch when he reroofed the house with standing seam copper.

The floor plan of the Griggs House is a large "L," with the inside of the "L" embracing the lawn and wooded creekside on the eastern part of the property, which was subdivided into a six-acre parcel soon after the house was built. This placement fulfilled one of Chauncey Griggs's requirements for the house: that it reflect the particulars of the climate of the Northwest, by welcoming the morning sun and turning its back on the rain from the west. He also wanted the house to have an open space big enough to accommodate his diverse collection of antique Japanese art and modern paintings, as well as host large gatherings for a wide variety of both live and recorded music.[8]

The Griggs House has 4,500 square feet of living space, making it one of Wright's largest post–World War II residences. Wright placed a row of 16-foot-tall plate glass windows along the east and south walls of the house, on the inner side of the "L," which provide lovely views of the sylvan setting. The tail of the "L" contains the living room and a bathroom, and the main entrance in the northeast corner of the house (there is also a picture glass doorway off the terrace). Wright originally planned for all the exterior walls of the house to be sheathed in peeled cedar logs. But he later changed his mind and used finely sawn cedar plank siding, which covers nearly

all the exterior except the east and south walls along the "L," where concrete pillars separate the tall picture glass windows. These planks are tilted upward at an angle that echoes the roofline above them.

Entering the Griggs House through the picture glass door on the terrace, the first thing one notices is the long, wide, light-filled gallery that runs the length of the central section. Here, Wright designed a soaring, 18-foot-high ceiling, with open beaming and wooden trusses. The sharp upward angle of this ceiling creates a very dramatic effect, and the space below it is perfect for entertaining large groups of people and has plenty of wall space for

FACING: Griggs House, living room with dining alcove. ABOVE: Griggs House, view of steeply pitched roofline.

displaying artwork. This is the widest gallery in any of Wright's Usonian houses, capable of holding 100 people quite comfortably.

To the right of the gallery is a wide dining alcove, with built-in window seats along the south and east walls. An open-hearth fireplace made of concrete blocks is set into the north wall of the dining alcove. Around the corner to the right is the living room, with a 16-foot-4-inch-tall walk-in fireplace set into the west wall, the tallest fireplace in any of Wright's West Coast houses. The ceiling of this room rises at a steep angle from north to south. The inner walls of both the dining room and living room are part of the

Griggs House, detail
of east façade.

Griggs House, view
from dining alcove.

massive masonry core at the heart of the home, a technique Wright had used since designing his earliest Prairie houses in the Midwest. The dining alcove has horizontal board-and-batten panels done in smooth-finished cedar along the outer walls, below the picture glass windows. At the top of these walls, Wright placed a clear glass clerestory, without the classic sawn wood geometric patterns that are found in most of his other Usonian houses on the West Coast. The floors throughout the house are made of concrete slabs, scored in a seven-by-seven-foot pattern, and stained lampblack.

To the left of the dining alcove, adjoining the gallery, is the service wing of the house, with the kitchen and pantry. This wing was expanded by Mark Griggs in recent years by pushing the north wall of the kitchen out eight feet. Beyond the gallery, in the west wing of the house, Wright placed five bedrooms, including a maid's room, with the master bedroom at the south end. There are three full baths and two half baths in the house. There was also a "freeze room" at the northwest corner of the house, which was originally designed for storing frozen foods but is now used as general storage space. After the house was completed, an additional room was added at the southwest corner, which is used as a sauna room. Wright placed his typical two-car carport adjacent to the north end of the house. As one crosses the wooden footbridge that Liddle designed over the creek and approaches the Griggs House from the east, it is easy to see why Wright considered this to be one of the most beautiful designs of his later career.

▼ ▼ ▼ ▼ ▼

Puget Sound is the largest inlet of the Pacific Ocean along the West Coast of the United States. It stretches for 100 miles from north to south: from the Strait of Juan de Fuca just below the Canadian border to Olympia, Washington. At its widest point just north of Seattle, it is about 20 miles across. At the high bluffs just south of Seattle, it is over six miles wide and approximately 600 feet deep.[9] Standing on the edge of these bluffs, over 100 feet above the azure waters below, you can look out across the forested hills of Vashon Island and beyond, to the snow-capped peaks of the Olympic Peninsula, 70 miles to the west. In this spectacular setting, Frank Lloyd Wright designed one of his most delightful residences for William and Elizabeth Tracy in 1955 in the community of Normandy Park, in what was then the southern fringes of Seattle.

Bill and Elizabeth Tracy were admirers of Frank Lloyd Wright's work; she was from Michigan and had visited Wright's 1939 Goetsch-Winckler House in Okemos. Elizabeth was a physical

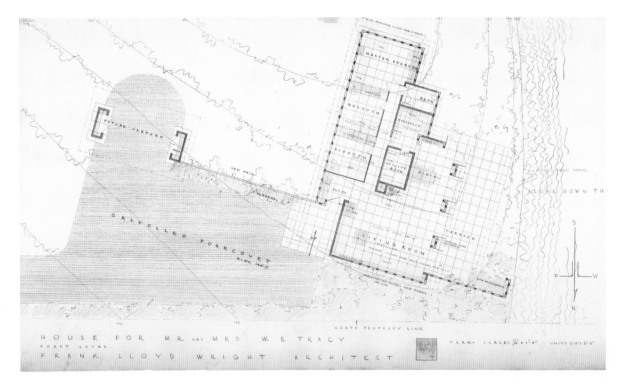

Tracy House, Normandy Park, Washington (1955), plot plan. Copyright © The Frank Lloyd Wright Foundation, Scottsdale, Arizona.

therapist and Bill was an engineer who had studied architecture. They moved to Washington State in the early 1950s, and soon afterwards they bought an approximately 31,000-square-foot, 100-foot-wide waterfront lot on the eastern edge of Puget Sound, about six miles south of Seattle.[10] The lot faces west, and when they bought it, it included a stand of mature trees, including towering Douglas firs and redwoods. It has panoramic views to the north, south, and

FACING: Tracy House, detail of west side with concrete blocks. ABOVE: Tracy House, east side.

west, overlooking some of the most spectacular natural scenery on the West Coast, with bald eagles flying overhead now and then.

When Bill and Elizabeth first contacted Wright about designing a house for them on their waterfront lot, he turned them down. However, they had become friends with a former apprentice of Wright's, Milton Stricker, who lived in the Seattle area, so they considered having him design their new home. But after he saw the site, he told them it was such a magnificent setting that Wright himself should design the house. He advised them to reapply and include photos of the site and surrounding natural features, as well as stating that they would use a local contractor named Ray Brandes, who had Wright design a home for him outside Seattle a few years earlier. After the Tracys followed Stricker's advice, Wright agreed to accept the commission. He soon produced a set of preliminary drawings, which Bill and Elizabeth approved with only very minor modifications. Wright then sent them a complete set of working drawings in spring 1955, and construction was completed in 1956.[11]

One of the reasons the Tracys were so eager to have Frank Lloyd Wright design their house was their interest in Wright's customized concrete block system of construction, a modification of his textile block system of the 1920s. He called this new variation the Usonian Automatic system, in which owners would take detailed plans he created for their special needs, then cast their own concrete blocks on the site for use in building their house. This system was developed in the early 1950s, when Wright came up with the idea of lighter, less-decorative hollow blocks than he had used in the 1920s. These blocks would be much less expensive, and it would be easier to knit them together using steel reinforcing rods and grouting. All the block joints had to be carefully measured so as to be exactly the same dimensions or an incremental error would accrue and throw off the entire wall they were part of. With Bill Tracy being an engineer, the Tracys felt they were up to the task of using this do-it-yourself system. They had the steel forms for the blocks made locally, and began casting two sets of blocks every day, five days a

FACING: Tracy House, view from entry hall past fireplace. ABOVE: Tracy House, view of dining room looking towards Puget Sound.

ABOVE: Tracy House, west façade with Puget Sound in distance. FACING: Brandes House, Sammamish, Washington (1952–53), east façade.

week. After several months of work, they had cast more than 1,700 blocks, enough to begin the construction of their home.[12] These blocks are rectangular shaped, with a recessed, or coffered, pattern.

The floor plan of the Tracy House is a single-story rectangle, with 1,150 feet of living space. The narrow front door is on the east side, with a set of raised concrete steps leading up to it at the end of a concrete pathway. To the left is a raised garden terrace set behind a retaining wall, and to the right is a detached carport. The house is set well back from the street to take full advantage of the view of Puget Sound, and provide maximum privacy. From the curb, the house appears to be an outcropping of its woodsy site, nestling comfortably into the earth and surrounding shrubbery.

To the left of the front door, inlaid into the lower wall, is a red square tile, a symbol Wright often used to mark a house as an authentic Wright design. The front door opens directly into the living room, with a dining area to the left. This is the largest space in the house, and Wright's use of floor-to-ceiling picture glass windows along the west wall gives it a light-filled, open feeling. These windows are separated by tall, thin columns of concrete blocks, which support the roof and create rhythm while allowing the magnificent views to be seen from every part of these two rooms. The living room has cushion-covered seats lining the north wall, with built-in bookshelves and redwood paneling above. Along the top of the north wall is a simple clerestory, much less decorative than those in most of his Usonian houses. At the corner of these two rooms is a fireplace, made of stacked concrete blocks. The dining area has the original table and chairs designed by Wright. There are two lights inserted into the concrete blocks lining the inner wall of this room, one on either side of the table, which provide soft lighting at night. The ceilings are eight feet six inches high, and made of the same coffered concrete blocks as the exterior walls. The floors throughout the house are made of concrete slabs in two-foot-wide patterns stained Cherokee red. There is a redwood-framed picture glass door at the southwest corner of the dining area that opens out onto a wide concrete terrace, providing an ideal setting to enjoy alfresco dining or just sit and soak up the natural beauty all around. Adjacent to the dining area is a small kitchen, located at the core of the house. There are three bedrooms along the east side of the house, connected by a narrow gallery, with the master bedroom at the south end. One of the most distinguishing features of the Tracy House is the columns of concrete blocks lining the west façade, which have glass bricks set into each row of blocks all the way up their length,

the top ones with lights inserted into them. These concrete blocks were painted off-white in the 1990s, but are being restored to their original sandy color.

Bill and Elizabeth Tracy lived happily in their Usonian Automatic house for the remainder of their lives (Bill died in 2009, and Elizabeth died in 2011). After Elizabeth's death the house was put on the market, and it eventually sold to a couple who have promised to retain all of its historic features.[13] The Tracy House was placed on the National Register of Historic Places in 1995. It is a superb example of Wright's later residential work, designed to be affordable and perfectly suited to its unique natural setting.

The lush green hills east of Seattle enfold several older communities that have become part of the metropolitan area without losing

their rustic character. One such community is Sammamish, a town of 45,000 people located 15 miles east of Seattle, that was an unincorporated part of King County in the 1950s. Here, hidden in the forested hills above Renton Issaquah Road, Frank Lloyd Wright designed one of the most elegant, aesthetically pleasing residences of his later career. The Ray Brandes House, designed in 1952, sits on the edge of a secluded glen in a three-and-a-half-acre lot bordered by Douglas firs, cedars, and other evergreen trees.

with Wright's work, having studied some of his Usonian homes, including the Goetsch-Winckler House in Okemos, Michigan. He also knew Wright's former apprentice, Milton Stricker. So Brandes wrote a letter to Wright asking him to design a single-story Usonian house for him and his wife, Mimi, including a detached workshop, with a two-car carport connecting the house and the shop. He wanted the home to have three bedrooms, since he and his wife planned to have children—although Mimi died before they

Above, left: Brandes House, east façade with entryway. Above, right: Brandes House, west façade with forest setting.

The property has retained its original pastoral character, so that this house appears to be sitting in the middle of its own private forest preserve, even though the lot was reduced from the 20 acres it once encompassed.

Ray Brandes was a Seattle-area building contractor, and his own house was the very first one he built. After completing his residence from Wright's design, he went on to build many architect-designed homes in the greater Seattle area. Brandes was familiar

could start a family.[14] What Wright designed for Ray Brandes was more than a customized Usonian house. Here he created a seamless synthesis of Prairie and Usonian elements, a harmonious blending of features from Wright's earliest and latest periods.

Approaching the Brandes House from the eastern side, what stands out the most is the horizontal, Prairie-style massing. The flat roof with wide, overhanging eaves that sweep across this façade, the banded, wood-frame plate glass windows along the upper walls, and the low horizontal profile of the building evoke some of Wright's Prairie homes in the Midwest. The front door opens directly into the living room, with the bedroom wing to the left and a long, narrow kitchen to the right. Thus the floor plan of this house is classic Usonian style. The kitchen still has its original stainless steel sink, stove, and countertops. The banded windows above the workspace admit ample natural light and provide views of the woods at the rear of the lot, giving the kitchen a pleasant

four-foot-wide square pattern, stained Cherokee red.

Entering the combination living room/library, visitors are struck by the graceful quality of this light, open, free-flowing space. Wright's tasteful use of warm redwood paneling along the north wall in the library nook, sand-colored concrete blocks on the exposed walls, and banded plate glass windows set into redwood framing along the west wall combine to create a feeling of elegance and sophistication. There is an open-hearth fireplace on the east wall, which is

ambience. A long, narrow gallery connects the three bedrooms in the south wing. These bedrooms have floor-to-ceiling plate glass doors on the west side, which open out onto the lush meadow in front. The walls in all three bedrooms and the gallery are paneled in smooth redwood lined with horizontal battens. There are also two small bathrooms in the south wing. The house has a total of 1,400 square feet of living space, laid out in the shape of a segmented rectangle. The walls are made of tiered rows of concrete blocks, and the floors throughout the house are concrete slabs in a

part of the masonry core of the house. There is a dining area to the right of the fireplace, where Wright placed a small, attached table, which still has the original wooden hassocks he designed for it. In the center of this open room, the ceiling is raised about a foot to create a light well, with a clerestory lined with an intricate sawn wood pattern. This same pattern was used on the clerestory above the built-in bookshelves in the library nook at the north end. Here Wright designed built-in seating along the wall, and Milton Stricker designed rectangular lights above the seats, which give off a warm

ABOVE: Brandes House, view of living room. FACING: Brandes House, view from living room to library alcove.

yellow glow. Down the center of the living room, or sitting room, as Ray Brandes liked to call it, Wright designed three pairs of wooden reading chairs, which flank small lamp tables. The Prairie-style lamps that stand next to these chairs are reproductions of earlier Wright-designed lamps, authorized by Taliesin.[15] Along the lower part of the south wall is a row of redwood cabinets. The most impressive feature of this room is the exquisite view of the forest-rimmed meadow as one looks west through the banded windows. A floor-to-ceiling glass-paneled door leads out to a concrete terrace that runs along the west façade of the house. The absolutely perfect siting and window placement of the Brandes House is all the more impressive when one considers that Wright designed it without ever having visited the lot. He drew the plans based solely on photos and topographical maps of the site, combined with his fertile imagination and his decades of experience. The construction was completed in late 1953.

The west façade of the Brandes House has wide overhanging eaves over a concrete slab terrace. The façade juts out along the living room wing at the point where it meets the bedroom wing. Over this jog in the terrace, Wright perforated the overhanging eaves with open trellising, much as he had done with the

FACING: Brandes House, details of eaves and roof trellis. ABOVE: Brandes House, kitchen. BELOW: Brandes House, view of gallery from bedroom.

213

Wright used the same distinctive geometric patterns along the clerestory that are found in the light well above the elegant living room/library. Here, as in all the residential rooms of the Brandes House, Wright applied the same attention to detail, and carefully chosen natural materials, that made him America's greatest architect.

▼ ▼ ▼ ▼ ▼

This journey through Frank Lloyd Wright's West Coast oeuvre, covering a distance of 1,500 miles and spanning the last 50 years of Wright's career, has provided us with abundant evidence that Wright was truly an innovator of twentieth-century modern architecture—or what today is called Midcentury Modern. Wright either invented or pioneered the use of many features that are now found on modern homes and public buildings around the world. These features include concrete slab floors, concrete block construction, carports, radiant heating systems, a concrete central utility core, walls of glass, free-flowing floor plans, and the combination living room/dining room.

This history of Wright's West Coast work also includes the untold stories of his professional relationships with several strong-willed and independent-minded female clients. These women, such as Aline Barnsdall and Della Brooks Walker, were able to get Wright to do something he was loath to do for most of his other clients. They were able to convince "the master" to make significant changes in his designs for their homes.

Those of us who live on the West Coast should count ourselves lucky that nearly all of Frank Lloyd Wright's public and private buildings in Washington, Oregon, and California remain standing—most of them intact and in their original setting. And for fans of Frank Lloyd Wright's work from around the world, they should be inspired by exploring the dozens of remaining examples of his structures on the West Coast, which are an invaluable part of his enduring legacy.

ABOVE: Frank Lloyd Wright. Courtesy of Hanna House Collection, sc0280. Department of Special Collections & University Archives, Stanford University Libraries, Stanford, California. FACING: Hanna House, Stanford, California (c. 1936–57), with stone lantern from Imperial Hotel in Tokyo, Japan.

Gordon House in Oregon. He also designed a distinctive geometric sawn wood pattern for the fascia, a classic Usonian feature.

The freestanding workshop is at the north end, and opens into the carport. Wright designed a finely finished interior for this space, with banded windows along the upper east wall that provide views of the nearby evergreen trees. There are built-in redwood cabinets, and the floor is made of the same two-foot-wide concrete slabs, stained Cherokee red, as the floors in the main house. A small, enclosed half bath fills the southeast corner, along with an open-hearth fireplace. The exterior has the same pattern of concrete block walls with tiered wood paneling at the corners as the exterior of the house does, and

APPENDIX

List of Frank Lloyd Wright's West Coast Buildings Open to the Public

Note: All of the residences featured in this book that are *not* listed below are occupied, so please respect the owners' privacy. Do not make an unannounced visit or take photos of these buildings while standing on the owners' property.

SOUTHERN CALIFORNIA

Anderton Court Shops, 332 North Rodeo Drive, Beverly Hills. The central ramp is open 24 hours a day; the adjacent shops are open during normal business hours, Monday through Saturday.

Barnsdall (Hollyhock) House, Barnsdall Art Park, 4800 Hollywood Boulevard, Los Angeles. As of this writing, the house is currently undergoing restoration, but is open for tours Friday through Sunday, 12:30 to 3:30 p.m. Call ahead for details. Fees: $7, general admission; $3, seniors; $2, youths under 17. Phone: (323) 644-6269.

Kundert Medical Clinic (now the offices of Dr. Kenneth Tway), 1106 Pacific Street, San Luis Obispo. Open Monday and Friday, 8:30 a.m. to 12 noon, and Tuesday through Thursday, 8:30 a.m. to 5:00 p.m. This is a working medical practice, so please act accordingly if you visit during business hours.

NORTHERN CALIFORNIA

Hanna House, 737 Frenchmans Road, Palo Alto (on the Stanford University campus). One-hour tours are given four times a month: each first and third Sunday, beginning at 11 a.m.; and each second and fourth Saturday at 11 a.m. Fee: $10 per person (does not include $5 campus parking permit). Phone: (650) 725-8352. Website: http://hannahousetours.stanford.edu/index.php?p=tinfo.

Marin County Civic Center, east on the San Pedro Road exit off Highway 101, San Rafael. The Administration Building is open for visitors Monday through Friday, 9 a.m. to 5 p.m.. Guided tours, beginning from room 233 on the second floor, are given each Wednesday at 10:30 a.m. Fee: $5 per person. Phone: (415) 473-3762. The Marin County Free Library (on the third floor of the Administration Building) is open Monday, Wednesday, and Friday, 10 a.m. to 6 p.m.; and Tuesday and Thursday, 10 a.m. to 9 p.m.

Pilgrim Congregational Church, 2850 Foothill Boulevard, Redding. Sunday services are 10 to 11:30 a.m. The building is otherwise open for visitors Monday through Thursday, 9 a.m. to 3 p.m., and Friday 9 a.m. to 12 p.m. Phone: (530) 243-3121. Ann Corrin, pastor.

V. C. Morris Gift Shop (now the Xanadu Gallery), 140 Maiden Lane, San Francisco. Open Tuesday through Saturday, 10 a.m. to 6 p.m. Phone: (415) 392-9999. Marsha Vargas Handley, owner.

OREGON

Gordon House, 869 West Main Street, Silverton, Oregon (on the grounds of the Oregon Garden). Open for tours Monday through Sunday, 12 to 4 p.m. Fee: $10 per person. Phone: (503) 874-6006. E-mail: gordonhouse1957@frontier.com. Molly Murphy, curator.

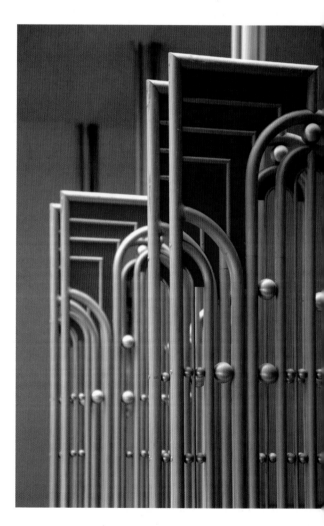

Marin County Civic Center, detail of entry-level staircase railings, Administration Building.

NOTES

INTRODUCTION

1. When a single date is given in parentheses following the name of a building, it refers to the year the building was completed; when a range of dates is given, they represent the year the building was designed followed by the year it was completed.

2. Deborah Vick (member-at-large, Frank Lloyd Wright Building Conservancy), interview by the author, January 2013, San Francisco.

3. Horace G. Simpson, "The Suburban Home—Its Design and Setting," *The Architect and Engineer of California* 44, no. 2 (February 1916): 44.

4. Robert C. Twombly, *Frank Lloyd Wright: His Life and His Architecture* (New York: John Wiley & Sons, 1979), 21.

5. "Biography," Frank Lloyd Wright, www.cmgww.com/historic/flw/bio.html; Vick, interview. Note that the figure on Wright's existing buildings includes the Feldman House in Berkeley, which was designed in 1938 but not built until 1974, after his death.

6. Donald C. Wilson, in discussion with the author, October 2005, Sacramento, CA. Actually, these students were incorrect in their description of this staircase, since it leads to an enclosed observation bubble that provides a view of the rooftop.

7. Comment by student, "Historic Architecture of the Bay Area" (class, Vista Community College, Berkeley, CA, November 1980).

8. Margaret Lins Stewart, telephone interview by the author, October 2012.

9. "The Envelope Please," *Architecture: The AIA Journal* 80, no. 10 (October 1991): 7.

CHAPTER 1

1. David Gebhard and Robert Winter, *A Guide to Architecture in Los Angeles & Southern California* (Salt Lake City: Peregrine Smith, 1982): 560.

2. "Historical Census Populations of Counties and Incorporated Cities in California, 1850–2010," California Department of Finance, www.dof.ca.gov/research/demographic/state_census_data_center/historical_census_1850-2010/view.php.

3. "Frank Lloyd Wright Designed Buildings: Stewart House," Waymarking.com, www.waymarking.com/waymarks/WMGD7_Stewart-house.

4. Michael Redmon, "Frank Lloyd Wright: Santa Barbara Is Home to One of the Architect's Designs," *Santa Barbara Independent,* October 10, 2011, www.independent.com/news/2011/oct/10/frank-lloyd-wright.

5. Ibid.

6. T. C. Boyle, e-mail to author, November 14, 2013.

7. T. C. Boyle, interview by the author, April 21, 2013, Montecito, CA.

8. Boyle, e-mail.

CHAPTER 2

1. "Hollywood," Wikipedia, http://en.wikipedia.org/wiki/Hollywood.

2. Jeffrey Herr, *Aline Barnsdall's Olive Hill Project* (Los Angeles: Angel City Press, 2005), 7.

3. Meryle Secrest, *Frank Lloyd Wright: A Biography,* new ed. (Chicago: University of Chicago Press, 1998), 266.

4. Herr, *Aline Barnsdall's Olive Hill Project,* 8.

5. "General Population by City: Los Angeles County, 1910–1950," Los Angeles Almanac, www.laalmanac.com/population/po26.htm.

6. Jeffrey Herr, interview by the author, April 19, 2013, Los Angeles.

7. William Allin Storrer, *The Architecture of Frank Lloyd Wright: A Complete Catalog,* 3rd ed. (University of Chicago Press, 2007), 180.

8. Herr, *Aline Barnsdall's Olive Hill Project,* 10.

9. Storrer, *Architecture of Frank Lloyd Wright,* 215.

10. Jeffrey Herr, e-mail to author, January 28, 2014.

11. Storrer, *Architecture of Frank Lloyd Wright,* 216.

12. Jeffrey Herr, e-mail to author, January 3, 2014.

13. Herr, *Aline Barnsdall's Olive Hill Project,* 9–10.

14. Storrer, *Architecture of Frank Lloyd Wright,* 216.

15. Ibid.

16. Herr, interview.

CHAPTER 3

1. David Gebhard, *The California Architecture of Frank Lloyd Wright* (San Francisco: Chronicle Books, 1997), 20.

2. Storrer, *Architecture of Frank Lloyd Wright,* 123.

3. Crosby Doe, interview by the author, April 21, 2013.

4. Storrer, *Architecture of Frank Lloyd Wright,* 219.

5. "Millard House," Wikipedia, http://en.wikipedia.org/wiki/Millard_House.

6. "Ennis House," Wikipedia, http://en.wikipedia.org/wiki/Ennis_House.

7. Storrer, *Architecture of Frank Lloyd Wright,* 222.

8. Char Miller, "Air Apparent: L.A.'s Bright Skies Are Not as Clear as They Seem," KCET: The Back Forty: Golden Green, May 1, 2013, www.kcet.org/news/the_back_forty/commentary/golden-green/airing-it-out.html.

9. "Ennis House," Wikipedia.

10. Ibid.

11. "No. 96 - Storer House," Big Orange Landmarks, December 17, 2007, http://bigorangelandmarks.blogspot.com/2007/12/no-96-storer-house.html.

12. "Storer House (Los Angeles)," Wikipedia, http://en.wikipedia.org/wiki/Storer_House_(Los_Angeles,_California).

13. Crosby Doe, interview by the author,

October 5, 2013.

14. "Storer House," Wikipedia.

15. Jeffrey M. Chusid, *Saving Wright: The Freeman House and the Preservation of Meaning, Materials, and Modernity* (New York: W. W. Norton, 2011), 228.

16. Ibid., 20–23.

17. Gebhard, *California Architecture of Frank Lloyd Wright,* 33.

18. Chusid, *Saving Wright,* 11, 17.

19. Ibid., 23–24.

20. *Frank Lloyd Wright,* DVD, directed by Ken Burns and Lynn Novick (PBS Home Video, 1998).

21. Trudi Sandmeier (director, Graduate Programs in Heritage Conservation, University of Southern California School of Architecture), interview by the author, October 16, 2013.

CHAPTER 4

1. "Frank Lloyd Wright Designed Buildings: Oboler Gatehouse and Retreat," Waymarking.com, www.waymarking. com/waymarks/WM1234.

2. Dorothy Knight, interview by the author, October 3, 2013.

3. Ibid.

4. "Oboler Gatehouse and Retreat," Waymarking.com.

5. Knight, interview.

6. Storrer, *Architecture of Frank Lloyd Wright,* 272.

7. Jack Larson, interview by the author, October 4, 2013.

8. Konrad Pearce, interview by the author, October 4, 2013.

9. Janet Bennett, "Frank Lloyd Wright House a Solar Wonder," *Star-News* (Pasadena, CA), March 14, 1974, http://newspaperarchive. com/star-news/1974-03-14/page-58.

10. Pearce, interview.

11. Ibid.

12. Ibid.

13. Storrer, *Architecture of Frank Lloyd Wright,* 320.

14. David Coffey (caretaker, George Ablin House), interview by the author,

October 6, 2013.

15. Letters and photographs on permanent display, George Ablin House, Bakersfield, CA.

16. Ibid.

17. Coffey, interview.

18. Storrer, *Architecture of Frank Lloyd Wright,* 428.

19. Coffey, interview.

20. Ibid.

CHAPTER 5

1. Mark Wilson, "Prairies Among the Redwoods," Hills Newspapers (Oakland, CA), real estate sec., June 29, 2001.

2. Ibid.

3. Larry Woodin, *The Maynard Buehler House* (pamphlet) (Chicago: Frank Lloyd Wright Building Conservancy, 2003).

4. Bob Ray (executor, Buehler Estate), interview by the author, November 2012, Orinda, CA.

5. Wilson, "Prairies Among the Redwoods."

6. Ibid.

7. Betty Olds (Walter Olds's widow), interview by the author, December 2012, Berkeley, CA.

8. Wilson, "Prairies Among the Redwoods."

9. Ibid.

10. Ray, interview.

11. Woodin, "The Maynard Buehler House."

12. Ray, interview.

13. Ibid.

CHAPTER 6

1. "Frank Lloyd Wright's Northern California Connection," *San Francisco Examiner,* April 10, 1959, editorial sec.

2. Mark Anthony Wilson, *Bernard Maybeck: Architect of Elegance* (Layton, UT: Gibbs Smith, 2011), 235 ch. 11, n. 15.

3. Julie Cain (project coordinator, Stanford Heritage Services), interview by the author, January 18, 2013, Stanford, CA.

4. Ibid.

5. Ibid.

6. Ibid.

7. Paul R. Hanna and Jean S. Hanna, *Frank Lloyd Wright's Hanna House: The Client's Report*

(New York: Architectural History Foundation/ Cambridge, MA: MIT Press, 1981), 51.

8. Ibid., 84.

9. Cain, interview.

10. Ibid.

11. "Hanna House," hannahousetours. stanford.edu.

12. Cain, interview.

13. "The House One Man Built," *Life,* December 28, 1959, 92.

14. *Romanza: The Structures of California Designed by Frank Lloyd Wright,* DVD, directed by Michael Miner (Reel Shop Productions, 2010).

15. Eric Berger, interview by the author, November 15, 2012, San Anselmo, CA.

16. Della Brooks Walker to Frank Lloyd Wright, June 13, 1945. Walker family letters collection.

17. Chuck Henderson (Della Walker's great-grandson), interview by the author, March 9, 2013, Carmel, CA.

18. Ibid.

19. Frank Lloyd Wright to Della Brooks Walker, February 27, 1951. Walker family letters collection.

20. Ibid.

21. Frank Lloyd Wright to Della Brooks Walker, March 21, 1952. Walker family letters collection.

22. Mary Walton, interview by the author, March 29, 2013, Modesto, CA.

23. Ibid.

24. Marc Grant, interview by the author, December 7, 2012, Berkeley, CA.

25. Storrer, 389.

CHAPTER 7

1. Bay Area Census: Marin County, www.bayareacensus.ca.gov/ counties/ MarinCounty.htm.

2. Chronology, newspaper clipping and pamphlet file, Anne T. Kent California Room, Marin County Free Library.

3. Ibid.

4. Susan Dinkelspiel Cerny, *An Architectural Guidebook to San Francisco and the Bay Area*

(Layton, UT: Gibbs Smith, 2007), 485.

5. Chronology, newspaper clipping and pamphlet file, Anne T. Kent California Room, Marin County Free Library.

6. "Frank Lloyd Wright to Design New Civic Center," *Marin Independent Journal,* June 27, 1957, 1.

7. Newspaper clipping and pamphlet file, Anne T. Kent California Room, Marin County Free Library.

8. *Marin Independent Journal,* August 1, 1957, 13.

9. Ibid., 14.

10. Ibid.

11. "Vets Object to Wright," *Marin Independent Journal,* July 26, 1957, 1.

12. "Wright Stalks Out of Board Meeting," *Marin Independent Journal,* August 2, 1957, 3.

13. Ibid., 4.

14. Ibid.

15. Ibid.

16. "Frank Lloyd Wright Discusses Plans for Marin Civic Center," *San Francisco Examiner,* August 3, 1957, 3–4.

17. Aaron G. Green with Donald P. DeNevi, *An Architecture for Democracy: The Marin County Civic Center* (San Francisco: Grendon Press, 1990), 94.

18. *Marin County Civic Center* (brochure published in conjunction with the dedication of the Marin County Civic Center Administration Building, San Rafael, CA, October 13, 1962) (Scottsdale, AZ: Frank Lloyd Wright Foundation, 1962).

19. "Wright Stalks Out of Board Meeting."

20. Frances O'Gara, "Red Charges Stir Wright to a Boil," *San Francisco Examiner,* August 3, 1957, 3.

21. William Earle, "Frank Lloyd Wright Unveils Marin Civic Center Plans," *Marin Independent Journal,* March 26, 1958, A-1.

22. Chronology, newspaper clipping and pamphlet file, Anne T. Kent California Room, Marin County Free Library.

23. Ibid.

24. Ed Montgomery, "Row Flares in Marin Over 'Taj Mahal,'" *San Francisco Examiner,* March 2, 1959, 1.

25. *Marin Independent Journal,* August 16, 1969.

26. Chronology, newspaper clipping and pamphlet file, Anne T. Kent California Room, Marin County Free Library.

27. Ibid.

28. Barry Spitz, *Marin: A History* (San Anselmo, CA: Potrero Meadow Press, 2006), 275.

29. Internet Movie Database, www.imdb.com.

30. "Marin Center Is a Thing of Beauty," *San Francisco Chronicle,* December 15, 1962, 44.

31. *Marin County Civic Center* (brochure).

CHAPTER 8

1. Storrer, *Architecture of Frank Lloyd Wright,* 313.

2. Robert McCarter, *Frank Lloyd Wright* (London: Phaidon Press, 1997), 307.

3. Ibid.

4. Marsha Vargas Handley (owner, Xanadu Gallery), interview by the author, January 22, 2013, San Francisco.

5. Ibid.

6. Ibid.

7. "Historical Census Populations of Counties and Incorporated Cities in California, 1850–2010," California Department of Finance, www.dof.ca.gov/research/demographic/state_census_data_center/historical_census_1850-2010/view.php.

8. Barbara Ashbaugh, *The Building of Pilgrim Congregational Church* (pamphlet) (Redding, CA: Pilgrim Congregational Church, 1992), 1.

9. Ibid., 3.

10. Ibid., 2.

11. Ibid.

12. Ann Corrin (pastor, Pilgrim Congregational Church), interview by the author, February 20, 2013, Redding, CA.

13. Ibid.

14. Vicky Tway (office manager, Kenneth P. Tway Clinic), interview by the author, April 18, 2013, San Luis Obispo, CA.

15. Ibid.

16. *History and Description of Kundert Medical Clinic* (San Luis Obispo, CA: San Luis Obispo County Historical Museum, n.d.).

17. Ibid.

18. "National Register of Historic Places Listings in Los Angeles County, California," Wikipedia, http://en.wikipedia.org/wiki/List_of_Registered_Historic_Places_in_Los_Angeles_County,_California.

19. "Anderton Court Shops," Wikipedia, http://en.wikipedia.org/wiki/Anderton_Court_Shops.

CHAPTER 9

1. Larry Woodin, *The Gordon House: A Moving Experience* (Hillsboro, OR: Beyond Words, 2002), 1–2; Molly Murphy (general director, Gordon House), interview by the author, July 24, 2013.

2. Woodin, *Gordon House: A Moving Experience,* 5.

3. Molly Murphy, interview.

4. "Eight Houses for Modern Living," *Life,* September 26, 1938, 60, http://books.google.com/books?id=f00EAAAAMBAJ&lpg=PP1&pg=PA45#v=onepage&q&f=false

5. Woodin, *Gordon House: A Moving Experience,* 18.

6. *The Gordon House* (brochure) (Silverton, OR: Gordon House).

7. Mark Griggs, interview by the author, July 22, 2013, Lakewood, WA.

8. Larry Woodin, interview by the author, July 23, 2013, Normandy Park, WA.

9. "Puget Sound," Wikipedia, http://en.wikipedia.org/wiki/Puget_Sound.

10. "The Tracy House," www.thetracyhouse.com/tth/Tracy_House/Tracy_House_files/Additional%20Information%20and%20Photos.pdf.

11. Ibid.; Larry Woodin, interview.

12. "The Tracy House."

13. Larry Woodin, interview.

14. Ibid.

15. Ibid.

BIBLIOGRAPHY

BOOKS AND MONOGRAPHS

Ashbaugh, Barbara. *The Building of Pilgrim Congregational Church* (pamphlet). Redding, CA: Pilgrim Congregational Church, 1992.

Boyle, T. C. *The Women*. New York: Viking, 2009.

Cerny, Susan Dinkelspiel. *An Architectural Guidebook to San Francisco and the Bay Area*. Layton, UT: Gibbs Smith, 2007.

Chusid, Jeffrey M. *Saving Wright: The Freeman House and the Preservation of Meaning, Materials, and Modernity*. New York: W. W. Norton, 2011.

Gebhard, David. *The California Architecture of Frank Lloyd Wright*. San Francisco: Chronicle Books, 1997. First published 1988 as *Romanza: The California Architecture of Frank Lloyd Wright* by Chronicle Books.

———, and Robert Winter. *A Guide to Architecture in Los Angeles & Southern California*. Salt Lake City: Peregrine Smith, 1982.

Green, Aaron G., with Donald P. DeNevi. *An Architecture for Democracy: The Marin County Civic Center*. San Francisco: Grendon Press, 1990.

Hanna, Paul R., and Jean S. Hanna. *Frank Lloyd Wright's Hanna House: The Client's Report*. New York: Architectural History Foundation/Cambridge, MA: MIT Press, 1981.

Herr, Jeffrey. *Aline Barnsdall's Olive Hill Project*. Los Angeles: Angel City Press, 2005.

History and Description of Kundert Medical Clinic. San Luis Obispo, CA: San Luis Obispo County Historical Museum, n.d.

Marin County Civic Center. Scottsdale, AZ: Frank Lloyd Wright Foundation 1962. Published in conjunction with the dedication of the Marin County Civic Center Administration Building, San Rafael, CA, October 13, 1962.

McCarter, Robert. *Frank Lloyd Wright*. London: Phaidon Press, 1997.

Spitz, Barry. *Marin: A History*. San Anselmo, CA: Potrero Meadow Press, 2006.

Secrest, Meryle. *Frank Lloyd Wright: A Biography*. Chicago: University of Chicago Press, 1998. First published 1992 by Knopf.

Storrer, William Allin. *The Architecture of Frank Lloyd Wright: A Complete Catalog*. 3rd ed. Chicago: University of Chicago Press, 2007.

———. *The Frank Lloyd Wright Companion*. Chicago: University of Chicago Press, 1993.

Twombly, Robert C. *Frank Lloyd Wright: His Life and His Architecture*. New York: John Wiley & Sons, 1979.

Wilson, Mark Anthony. *Bernard Maybeck: Architect of Elegance*. Layton, UT: Gibbs Smith, 2011.

Woodin, Larry. *The Gordon House: A Moving Experience*. Hillsboro, OR: Beyond Words, 2002.

———. *The Maynard Buehler House* (pamphlet). Chicago: Frank Lloyd Wright Conservancy, 2003.

ARTICLES

Earle, William, "Frank Lloyd Wright Unveils Marin Civic Center Plans," *Marin Independent Journal,* March 26, 1958, A-1.

Simpson, Horace G. "The Suburban Home—Its Design and Setting." *The Architect and Engineer of California* 44, no. 2 (February 1916): 39–45.

Wilson, Mark. "Prairies Among the Redwoods." Hills Newspapers (Oakland, CA), real estate sec., June 29, 2001.

"The Envelope Please." *Architecture: The AIA Journal* 80, no. 10 (October 1991): 7.

"The House One Man Built." *Life,* December 28, 1959, 92.

"Frank Lloyd Wright to Design New Civic Center." *Marin Independent Journal,* June 27, 1957, 1.

"Wright Stalks Out of Board Meeting." *Marin Independent Journal,* August 2, 1957, 3.

"Frank Lloyd Wright Discusses Plans for Marin Civic Center." *San Francisco Examiner,* August 3, 1957, 3–4.

"Marin Civic Center Final Plans Approved." *San Francisco Examiner,* March 2, 1959.

"Frank Lloyd Wright's Northern California Connection." *San Francisco Examiner,* editorial sec., April 10, 1959.

AUDIOVISUAL MATERIAL

Frank Lloyd Wright. Directed by Ken Burns and Lynn Novick. PBS Home Video, 1998.

The Homes of Frank Lloyd Wright. A&E Home Video, 1996.

Romanza: The Structures of California Designed by Frank Lloyd Wright. Directed by Michael Miner. Reel Shop Productions, 2010.

INDEX

Note: **Boldfaced** page numbers indicate illustrations.

161–162; site inspection by Wright, 149–150; "space age" appearance, 162; Spanish Colonial features of, 151; spire-shaped tower, **152**, 153, 155, **158**, 162, **165**; UNESCO World Heritage list, 10; Vera Schultz's support for Wright, 9, 146, **147**, 148, 150, 159; Wright commissioned to design, 145; Wright on, 146, **151**, 158–159, 164; Wright signs contract to design, 150; Wright's death prior to construction, 159

Marin County Civic Center Library (San Rafael, California), 151, 153, 155, **159**

Marin Veterans Memorial Auditorium, 158, 160, **161**

Marshall, James, 159

Martin, Ricky, 42

Masselink, Eugene, 81

Mathews House (Atherton, California), 112–113, **112–113**

Matsutani, Henry, 91

Matthews, J. B., 148

Mayan and pre-Columbian style: cross motifs in, 38; Ennis House, 8, **12**, **41**, 41–42, **42–43**, 44, 44–45, **45**; Freeman House, **53**, **54**, 54–56, **55**, **56**, **57**; Millard House, **7**, **34**, 35–36, **36**, **37**, **38**, 38–39, **39**, 40, 41, **41**; Storer House, **46**, 46–47, **47**, **48**, 49, **49**, 50, **51**, **52**, 53; Wright's first uses of, 26–27. *See also* Barnsdall (Hollyhock) House

"Mayan Revival" style, 41

Maybeck, Bernard, 15, 97, 174

McCarthy, Joseph, 148

McClain, James, 161–162

Meyers Medical Clinic (Dayton, Ohio), 179

Midcentury Modern style, 214

Millard, Alice and George, 35, 39

Millard House (Pasadena, California), **7**, **34**, 35–36, **36**, **37**, **38**, 38–39, **39**, 40, 41, **41**

Morgan, Julia, 174, 179

Morris, Mr. and Mrs. V. C., 167

movie and TV series productions: Ennis House, 8, 42; Marin County Civic Center, 162; Oboler Compound, 65; Pearce House, 69; Walker House, 8, 119

music videos, 42, 162

N

National Register of Historic Places: Anderton Court Shops, 184; Gordon House, 196; Hanna House, 107; Millard House, 38; Storer House, 53; Tracy House, 207

neo-Gothic style, 27

Nesbit, John, 44

Neutra, Richard, 15, 32, 56, 145, 146

Nissan Motor Company, 107

Noel, Miriam, 28

Northridge earthquake of 1994, 32, 45

O

Oboler, Arch and Eleanor, 59–60, 63, 65, 66

Oboler Compound (Malibu, California), **58**, **59**, 59–61, **60**, **61**, **62**, 63, **63**, **64**, **65**, 65–66, **66**

O'Keeffe, Georgia, 186

Olds, Walter, 89, 92–94, 172

Oregon Garden, 191, 196

organic design philosophy, 8, 10, 98, 119, 122, 146, 151

Owen, Andrew L., 92

P

Pauson House (Phoenix), 60

Pearce, Konrad, 69, 74, 75

Pearce, Llewellyn, 75

Pearce, Wilbur C. and Elizabeth, 69–70, 74, 75

Pearce House (Bradbury, California), 69–70, **70**, **71**, **72**, **73**, **74**, 74–75, **75**

Period Revival style, 10

Permanent Midnight (movie), 69

Peters, William Wesley "Wes," 70, 75, 81, 105, 132, 159, 160

Peterson, Jerald, 21

Picasso, Pablo, 13, 186

Pilgrim Congregational Church (Redding, California), **174**, 174–175, **175**, **176–177**, 177–179, **178**, 216

Pleasence, Donald, 162

pole and boulder Gothic style, **174**, 174–175, **175**

Ponce de Leon Hotel (St. Augustine, Florida), 35

Prairie School movement, 10–11

Prairie style: in Barnsdall (Hollyhock) House, 27, 31; in Brandes House, 208–209, 213; in Chicago residences, 10; criticized by established architects, 10–11; features of, 10, 16, 19, 31; in Griggs House, 201; in Hanna House, 97; and Romanesque arches, 167; in Stewart House, 8, 15, 16, 19, 21; in Unity Temple, 173

pre-Columbian style. *See* Mayan and pre-Columbian style

Price, Vincent, 42

Puttnam, Tony, 177

R

radiant heating system, 92, 134, 193

Rains, Claude, 56

Rattenbury, John, 177

Ray, Bob, 94

real estate development, Wright on, 146–147

Reinhardt, Bryson, 147–148

religious structures: Pilgrim Congregational Church, **174**, 174–175, **175**, **176–177**, 177–179, **178**, 216; variety of Wright's commissions on, 173–174

Replacement Killers, The (movie), 42

Residence A (Los Angeles), 31, **32**

Residence B (Los Angeles), 31, 32

Rice, Condoleezza, 107

Robie House (Chicago), 8, 10, **10**, 21

Romanesque arches, 167, 168, **168**

"Romanza" architecture, 8

Rush Hour (movie), 42

S

San Francisco: V. C. Morris Gift Shop, 89, 97, 113, **166**, 167–169, **168**, **169**, **170**, **171**, **172**, 172–173, **173**, 216; Wright on, 97; Wright's office in, 97

San Rafael, California: as setting for Marin County Civic Center, 145–146; Wright on, 146–147, 150, 164

Santa Barbara, economic boom in, 15

Saving Wright (book), 54

Schindler, Pauline, 53

Schindler, Rudolph, 31, 32, 53, 55, 56

Schubart, Henry, 146

Schultz, Vera, 9, 146, **147**, 148, 150, 159

Schwartz House (Two Rivers, Wisconsin), 191

Shasta College, 174

Silver, Joel, 53

Simon and Garfunkel, 13

Simpson, Horace G., 10

Smith, David and Carey, 194, 196

Smith, George Washington, 15

"So Long, Frank Lloyd Wright" (song), 13

Space Age style, 186, **187**

Spanish Colonial architecture, 151

spiral ramp design, **166**, 167, 168, **170**

spires: Anderton Court Shops, 184, **184**, **185**, 186, **186**; Marin County Civic Center (San Rafael, California), **152**, 153, 155, **158**, 162, **165**

Stanford University, 97, 98, 107

"starkitecture," 143

Stewart, George and Emily, 15, 21

Stewart, Margaret Lins, 13

Stewart House (Montecito, California): cruciform floor plan of, 16, **17**; description of, 16–17, 19, 21; first California commission for Wright, 15, 22; nicknamed "Butterfly Woods," 16; photo of,